M.
Dev
foster.

Acknowledgements

I would like to thank the Social Services Department of the City of Newcastle upon Tyne for enabling me to pursue the empirical research which formed the basis of the study. Special thanks are due to the foster carers and social workers who gave their time to complete the questionnaires, and to my colleagues in the Adoption and Fostering Unit for their support, especially Mr Alan Jackson.

I am particularly indebted to Dr Peter Selman of the Department of Social Policy, University of Newcastle upon Tyne who, as my supervisor, was extremely generous in giving me time, advice, guidance and support. In addition the study benefited from the advice and assistance of several members of the Department of Social Policy. Further thanks must go to the academics and researchers whom I consulted in carrying out the research, in particular Jane Rowe and David Berridge, who were generous in giving me their time, knowledge, advice and encouragement. Thanks also go to Northumberland Social Services Department for help in providing data and support.

Last, but not least, I am extremely grateful for the advice, guidance and assistance that I have received in preparing the study for publication – to June Thoburn for encouragement and valuable comments and suggestions, and to Pete Bentley and Shaila Shah from BAAF who read the manuscript and provided help, advice and sometimes inspiration, in the final stages.

It goes without saying, nevertheless, that responsibility for errors and omissions is entirely my own.
Judith Stone

Note

Judith Stone has worked in child care social work for fifteen years, both in the UK and overseas, and currently works for Northumberland Social Services Department as Development Worker for the Children's Services Division. Prior to this she was a Training Officer for Northumberland and a Research Associate at the University of Newcastle upon Tyne. She was awarded the degree of M. Phil in Social Policy in 1993 for the research upon which this study is based, and which was undertaken when she was a Social Worker in the Adoption and Fostering Unit of Newcastle upon Tyne Social Services. A copy of the questionnaire is available for perusal in Stone, J, *Children in Care: the Role of Short-Term Fostering*, unpublished M.Phil thesis, University of Newcastle upon Tyne, 1992, in the Robinson Library, University of Newcastle upon Tyne, or through inter-library loan.

Making Positive Moves
Developing short-term fostering services

Judith Stone

British
Agencies
for **A**doption
and **F**ostering

Published by
British Agencies for Adoption & Fostering
(BAAF)
Skyline House
200 Union Street
London SE1 0LX
Registered Charity 275689

© BAAF 1995

**British Library Cataloguing in Publication
Data**
A CIP catalogue record for this book is
available from the British Library
ISBN 1 873868 18 9

Designed by Andrew Haig & Associates
Typeset, printed and bound by Russell Press
(TU) in Great Britain

Contents

Foreword

When invited by local authorities to discuss their 'permanence' policies I have often found it necessary to stress that an effective foster care service is essential if children are to be successfully placed back home or with permanent substitute families. Without skilled temporary carers, who could be residential workers but will most often be foster carers, who can give high quality care, sometimes therapy and certainly warmth and affection for as long as it takes to find the right placement, it is inevitable that a greater proportion of permanent placements will break down. Yet, leaving aside specialist schemes, short term foster care was, in the 1980s, the most neglected aspect of child and family social work both by researchers and by those who wrote about practice. Apart from the small number of short term placements evaluated by Berridge and Cleaver in 1987[1] and the important information in Rowe et al's *Child Care Now*[2] survey of the extent and aims of this form of placement, short term foster care was a side issue, if that, in most books about child care services.

Happily the Children Act has brought renewed interest in the subject, and 1995 has seen the publication of the first practice text for many years which focuses on the theory and practice of foster care.[3] Judy Stone's work will be another important addition. She undertook her research in Newcastle just as the Act was being implemented. It is to the credit of that Authority that they were one of a small number of Social Services Departments who had the foresight to do then what many authorities are just coming round to, and encourage a member of staff to undertake a study of their short term foster care service. It is essentially a survey of a cohort of 183 placements with basic details taken from records and supplemented by more detailed information from the social workers of 104 of them. As such it paints only one side of the picture and can usefully be complemented by Sellick's[4] set of interviews with short term foster carers themselves, and by the consumer views reported by other researchers and summarised in the two Department of Health reviews of research.

However, the picture of the case held by social workers at the time of placement is, or at least was then, essentially the picture on which the decisions about placement were based. It will be interesting to see whether the Children Act requirement to consult the wishes and feelings of parents and children and to give them due consideration has led to a fuller picture being obtained before placement.

The report of the research provides information about the children and their families, and about the aims of these temporary foster placements in the context of broader social work interventions. It attempts to tease out characteristics of those who stayed longer and those who returned home quickly, and of the placements which failed to last as long as needed. In common with other researchers Judy Stone found that the widespread belief that if you let them into care you will have a hard job to get them out again was ill-founded for the majority, since 70 per cent were home within three months. She helpfully picks out that it is the 10 to 14 year olds who are most likely to be 'long-stayers'. The majority of children who moved on did so to a, hopefully, permanent placement at home, in independent living or with a substitute family; fifteen per cent were long stayers in the same temporary placement. Some would use the label 'drift' for these, but the interview material indicates that their cases were complex and that there was usually much activity to make more appropriate permanent arrangements. The group which should worry us are the 12 per cent who moved on to another temporary placement, and the, to some extent overlapping, 13 per cent who moved to this short term placement from another placement in care. Amongst the many questions Judy Stone poses for us I would pick out – could the movement within temporary care of the first group be avoided, and could we predict who the long stayers might be, and thus take extra care to ensure that we get the right temporary placement to meet their needs until more permanent arrangements are arrived at? The overall impression is that, leaving aside infants going on to uncontested adoption, the small but important minority who do not return home quickly will need an intermediate length placement able to meet their needs for a flexible period of at least six months and up to two years.

Readers will, I hope, use this study to reflect on questions for which they are seeking answers in their own areas, or on issues which are the subject of more general debate. There are few surprises about the parents and children, with poverty and material disadvantage and disability interwoven with relationship difficulties. Children of mixed ethnicity are again over-represented. I was interested to note that even before the Children Act was implemented, 'voluntary care' was used extensively in Newcastle as a support service to families, and also for children who might broadly be described as 'in need of protection'. I also particularly welcomed the section on the fathers' views about the placement. Although they were frequently absent form the households and the planning, they at least got a mention in the research. The majority of cases were already open to social workers so it is sad to note that several years after Packman's study,[5] and in an authority which looked favourably on the provision of family support services, in the minds of some workers or team managers, foster placement was unthinkable 'until it became too late to think at all'. No doubt these cases were amongst the fifth who moved to the short term placement in an 'emergency' without a clear plan or set of aims.

To conclude, I am sure that you will find in this study much of relevance to your day to day work as practitioners, planners, managers or educators. As a bonus, Judy Stone has provided a comprehensively updated account of the research on child placement, which she helpfully interweaves with her study findings.

I hope that this detailed and carefully researched study will throw some light on the dilemmas you are meeting in your own practice, and if you don't find the answers you are looking for, that you will ensure that your agency undertakes its own research and makes it widely available. There is a long way to go before we will know as much about short-term placements as we need to know if the thousands of children who use them each year are to get an improved service. In providing this account of short-term foster placements just before the Children Act was implemented Judy Stone has offered a baseline and set us off in the right direction.

June Thoburn
University of East Anglia
April 1995

References

1   Berridge D, and Cleaver H, *Foster Home Breakdown*, Blackwell, 1987.

2   Rowe J, Hundleby M, and Garnett L, *Child Care Now*, BAAF, 1989.

3   Triseliotis J, Sellick C, and Short R, *Foster Care: Theory and practice*, Batsford/BAAF, 1995.

4   Sellick C W, *Supporting Short Term Foster Carers*, Avebury, 1992.

5   Packman J, *Who Needs Care*, Blackwell, 1992.

Introduction

This study explores the service provided by short-term foster carers, investigating the functions they perform, and describing the children and families using the placements. It highlights the distinctiveness of this service which has hitherto gone largely unrecognised, but which has over recent years emerged in its own right as a significant part of public child care provision.

The study of short-term fostering is long overdue, but the implementation of the Children Act 1989 has provided new impetus to investigate the organisation and provision of services to children and families which gather together under the broad descriptive term "short-term foster care", and to evaluate the part to be played by these services in relation to the aims of the new Act. The Children Act 1989 created a new system of child care provision, and new challenges and opportunities for all involved in providing public child care services. This has necessitated a fresh look at existing practices in the light of the aims and goals of the new Act, to evaluate how far services need to be developed to meet the new legislative requirements, both in the Act itself and in the accompanying Regulations and Guidance. The necessity to evaluate and plan services for children and families is being given added impetus with the development of Children's Services Plans – documents produced by social services departments detailing plans for services for children. This study provides an opportunity to evaluate short-term foster care, and to consider how it could develop further to assist children and their families in different ways.

Short-term family placement appears to be growing in importance. In their study titled *Child Care Now*[1] Rowe et al identified a trend towards an increasing number of short placements. This seems to have accelerated following the implementation of the Act in October 1991. Table 1 shows figures derived from Northumberland County Council which show that whilst family placements overall have risen only slightly, there is a noticeable trend towards an increasing number of short-term foster placements, and a decrease in the number of long-term placements.

The starting point for this study was an examination of 183 short-term foster placements in Newcastle upon Tyne which, for the first time, provided a detailed analysis of how short-term foster homes were being used in day to day social work in a local authority social services department. Although the study was carried out before the implementation of the Children Act 1989 in England and Wales, the findings have an important bearing on present day practice. Nothing had been written about either the organisation of these services, or how they might best meet the demands being placed upon them; the research study arose as an attempt to fill these gaps.

Since the study began prior to the implementation of the Children Act 1989, it spans a period of major legislative change, involving new legal orders, terminology, concepts and principles. Where research data was collected before the new Act was implemented, it has been necessary to continue to use terminology relevant to the old legislation. Elsewhere terminology is consistent with the current legal framework of the Children Act 1989. A glossary is provided to explain terms used under both legal systems (see Appendices).

The need for the study

Up to now there has been relatively little specific research interest in short-term fostering. Triseliotis[2] noted in 1989 that major studies which appeared before 1985 concentrated on long-term foster care and that short-term foster care was one of the least researched types of fostering. Berridge and Cleaver[3] studied foster home breakdown in the mid 1980s and did include an investigation of short-term fostering, providing the first detailed study. They reported in 1987 that they had been 'unable to reveal any previous major study of this area'.

Although short-term foster care has been neglected in research studies, its importance is increasing and its distinctive contribution becoming more apparent. There are now a number of specific opportunities and problems presented by short-term foster care services: it is an area of growing significance in child care work; there has been growing interest

Table 1

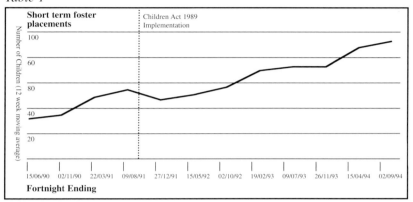

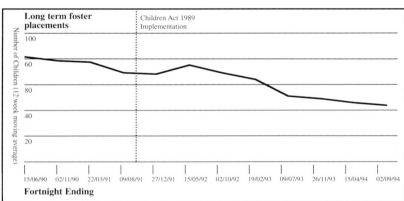

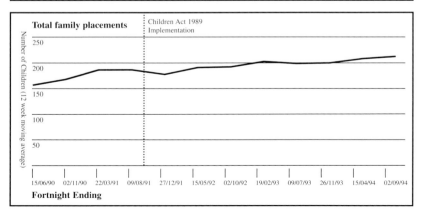

in the positive use of short-term care; but short-term placements often last longer than expected. These are briefly described below and examined in greater detail in Chapter 1.

Short-term foster care is likely to be a child's first experience of care. These first few weeks in care have been shown to be crucial in the development of a child's care "career".[4] Recent research studies[5,6,7,8,9] placed a spotlight upon the early days and weeks in care, and the quality of the service provided at this point is crucial. Earlier studies[10,11] had found it was quite common for short-term placements to become long-term. As early as 1953, Bowlby recorded the view that 'A long-stay case is generally a short-stay case that has been mishandled'.[12] The findings of a number of recent research studies[13] have indicated that social work activity in the early weeks of care is crucial in effecting a speedy return home and tend to give credence to Bowlby's assertion. The importance of short-term foster care, and its vital role in determining the child's future, has certainly become more apparent. Short-term foster homes have become the focus of a period of intensive work – contact, planning meetings, reviews, and possibly court hearings have been added to the basic task of caring for the child, thereby placing extra demands on foster carers.

Since the *Review of Child Care Law*[14] in 1985 there has been greater interest in the positive use of short-term care as a service for families in the prevention of family breakdown. The messages from a number of research studies completed in the early 1980s were summarised by the DHSS in 1985 in *Social Work Decisions in Child Care*,[15] which identified the 'potentialities of using short-term care as a means of preventing the permanent break-up of families by offering temporary relief'. This became one of the underpinning principles of the Children Act 1989:

'*A wide variety of services, including short-term out-of-home placements may need to be employed in order to sustain some families through particularly difficult periods.*'[16]

Chapter 2 examines the historical context of short-term foster care, and provides evidence that short-term foster care has indeed been used since the 1950s to provide relief to families experiencing difficulties and problems caring for their children. However, because of lack of resources, it has been difficult to meet requests for local foster carers; for children to return to foster carers they know; to provide, and stick to, planned episodes of respite care; or to retain foster carers for this purpose.

The possibilities of using short-term foster care in this way have been increased since the implementation of the Children Act 1989, which introduces under Part III, Section 20, the provision of "accommodation" as a service to the families of children in need, while they retain full parental responsibility, and allows for a series of short placements with the same foster carer to be treated as one placement provided they meet certain criteria. In the past few years this pattern of respite care has been particularly developed to provide services to parents who have children with severe learning or physical disabilities. Aldgate, Bradley and Hawley[17] at the University of Oxford have undertaken a study of the current operation of respite care and consider how effectively these services could be expanded to the families of other children who are in touch with social services. Their research suggests that the delivery of respite care demands careful attention to details of practice and organisation of services, but shows the variety of respite care that can be developed within the personal social services.

A number of short-term foster placements, however, last considerably longer than expected. Researchers acknowledge that this is a problem, and represents a form of breakdown.[18,19] Children can stay in short-term foster homes literally for years rather than weeks. This places a strain on the children, their parents and the foster carers. Foster carers may not have been adequately prepared or recruited for the task, and problems can arise when children, who have made significant attachments to temporary carers, have to move on or return home.

Both Berridge and Cleaver as well as Rowe et al expressed concern that short-term foster care could perhaps be *too* "successful", in that, in a sixth to a quarter of all cases studied, children remained much longer than was envisaged.[20,21] Berridge and Cleaver were the first to consider whether a placement that lasts significantly longer than intended also signifies a form of breakdown in the social work plan. They found that 28 per cent of the children were still in the same placement at six months, and 14 per cent were still there after a year. A quarter of these eventually resulted in a crisis with the foster carers insisting on the child's removal, but none returned immediately to their birth family.[22] The *Child Care Now* study[23] reported in 1989 that 15 per cent of the placements under examination lasted longer than planned, and Millham et al[24] had also noted in 1986 that temporary placements of children could persist longer than intended and that this often resulted in ad hoc decisions concerning the child's welfare.

Another area of concern has been the short-term fostering of adolescents. Berridge and Cleaver's study[25] in the mid 1980s included a small number of foster placements involving adolescents, and found them to be the age group experiencing the least successful placements, with seven out of 18 breaking down, and rarely resulting in a return to the birth family. *Child Care Now* found youngsters in their mid-teens were the most vulnerable to placements ending prematurely.[26] Correspondingly, Thorpe and Bilson[27] showed in 1987 that the children who drift long-term in the care system are primarily adolescents.

It is evident that short-term fostering is a key service that is currently required to perform a range of different functions. Although it first emerged as a service largely to meet the needs of parents unable to look after their children during a period of illness, or confinement, or similar short-term difficulty, it has developed into a much more complex provision, firmly enmeshed in the wider child care scene. This study aims to identify these different functions and explore how short-term foster care may be used to meet the requirements of the Children Act 1989.

When the Children Act 1989 was placed on the statute books, government guidance indicated that it both *reflected* and *required* changes in practice.[28] It is necessary to take stock and ask important questions about existing short-term placement provision, in order to be better able to plan for the future. Volume 3 of the Regulations and Guidance makes it clear that it is no longer enough to classify placements into categories of "short-term" and "long-term", and urges social workers to be at once more flexible and more precise:

> *'Short-term, respite, and long-term placement are convenient descriptive terms and are used as such in this Guidance. They are insufficiently precise, however, for the purposes of planning for individual children. Planning needs to address the aim of the placement, and specific tasks associated with the aim, and the expected duration of the placement.'*[29]

This study helps to clarify the nature of existing short-term foster care provision, including the length, aims and objectives, and outcomes of placements, and concludes with recommendations as to where more flexible and differentiated services could be provided to meet children's different needs and those of their families.

The impact of the Children Act 1989

The framework within which short-term foster care is offered to children and families in England and Wales is now provided by the Children Act 1989. Clearly, one of the most fundamental changes brought about by the Act is in relation to the provision of care and maintenance for children by local authorities. In this regard both the concepts and terminology used have been radically changed.

Previously all children provided with care and maintenance were officially "in care". Now all children provided with care and maintenance for more than 24 hours are "looked after", but only children on legal orders are deemed to be "in care". The Act replaces parental rights with the concept of "parental responsibility", which comprises 'all the rights, duties, powers, responsibilities, and authority which by law a parent has in relation to the child' (Section 3(1)). Unlike parental rights, parental responsibility is enduring and can be shared (Section 2.5). Consequently, a person does not cease to have parental responsibility for a child solely because someone else acquires it. In fact, parental responsibility is only extinguished by an adoption order.

Children who would formerly have been in "voluntary care" (under Section 2 of the Child Care Act 1980), can be voluntarily "accommodated" under Section 20, Part III of the Act, whilst their parents retain full parental responsibility for them. The arrangement is entirely voluntary, and is now seen as a service providing positive support to the child and his or her family, and can be terminated by a person with parental responsibility at any time. That this is quite a radical departure from practice under previous legislation was stressed in 1991 in *Patterns and Outcomes in Child Placement*:[30]

> *'The greatest change will be in relation to children for whom "accommodation" is provided. This replaces the status of voluntary*

care in earlier legislation and in these cases the authority will be accountable to the parents. This new relationship and change in the balance of power requires a radical shift in thinking on behalf of both administrators and social workers.'

The Children Act 1989 includes a range of new duties and powers to provide accommodation for children of all ages. Volumes 2 and 3 of the Guidance and Regulations spell out the details of the services to be provided in this respect. Volume 2 stresses the shift in emphasis that needs to be brought about because of the change from voluntary care to the provision of accommodation under Part III, which is not to be seen as a last resort, occasioned by parental shortcomings, but as a means of identifying and providing for a child's needs. It aims to be a positive response, with no fear of stigma or loss of parental responsibility. It requires that children and parents are consulted about decisions, and that wherever possible and desirable, children should be placed locally and brothers and sisters placed together.

For the first time in child care legislation the Children Act 1989 takes into account the multi-ethnic and multi-cultural nature of society in the UK. It is now a requirement of the Children Act 1989, Section 22(5)(c) that 'before making any decision with respect to a child whom they are looking after, or proposing to look after . . . a local authority shall give due consideration . . . to the child's religious persuasion, racial origin and cultural and linguistic background.' These are matters that must be considered before a decision about placement is made. In addition, Volume 3, 2.62 advises that the contents of the plan for a "looked after" child should contain, as one of the key elements, the child's identified needs (including needs arising from race, culture, religion or language, special educational or health needs). Under the Act local authorities must also consider the ethnic groups in the local community when recruiting foster carers.

Volume 3 (2.40, 2.41, 2.42) provides more specific guidance in relation to how these requirements are to be carried out in providing placements for children under the Act. It makes it clear that the guiding principle of good practice is that a placement with a family of similar ethnic origin and religion is most likely to meet a child's needs as fully as possible and to safeguard his or her welfare most effectively. Guidance and Regulations (Volume 3, para 4.4) emphasises 'that a child's need for continuity in life and care should be a constant factor in choice of placement. In most cases this suggests a need for placement with a family of the same race, religion, and culture in a neighbourhood within reach of family, school or day nursery, church, friends and leisure activities.'

This is just as important in short-term as in long-term placements, as Hammond stresses:

> 'For children who are in care temporarily the value to them and their families of a familiar environment should not be underestimated both in coping with the trauma of separation or in aiding the process of reuniting the family.'[31]

Families from a similar ethnic background who share a common heritage, including common expectations of parent–child relationships and behaviour, will more often be able to work with birth parents in an "inclusive" fostering model.[32] This too should increase the chances of a successful return home for the child.

However, as already mentioned, placements can last considerably longer than planned. The problems associated with transracial short-term placements become particularly acute when after months or years in a temporary placement, and when attachments between children and carers become strong, decisions have to be made about permanent substitute care. A typical example which hit the headlines in August 1989 was a situation in Croydon. A black baby had been placed with white short-term foster carers, but the placement lasted over two years, by which time attachments had formed between the child and the foster carers. They wished to keep him when it was decided he needed a permanent placement. This conflicted with Croydon's policy not to place black children with white permanent substitute families. The child's need for a same race placement then had to be balanced against his need to remain with the family to whom he had become attached, a situation where it seemed impossible to meet all the child's needs, and which created a great deal of conflict.[33,34]

The Act requires that decisions are taken on an individual basis to ensure that the welfare of each child in relation to their racial origin and culture is adequately met alongside their needs in other respects. There is little research to inform these decisions in relation to short-term foster care. A discussion of the issues is included in Chapter 1. A small number of black and minority ethnic children were included in this study, but the sample was too small to analyse separately. However, these placements are examined in more detail in Chapter 6 which looks at the specific needs of the black and minority ethnic children in short-term foster care in this sample.

Very importantly, there is the requirement to consult and have due regard to the wishes and feelings of both children and parents in relation to any child whom the local authority is looking after or proposes to look after; Volume 3 makes explicit the need to provide children with guidance and counselling to enable them to consider their wishes very carefully.

The Children Act 1989 has also introduced the completely new concept of "children in need". These are children unlikely to achieve or maintain a reasonable standard of health or development, or whose health or development would be significantly impaired, without the provision of services; and children who are disabled (Section 17(10)). Furthermore, the Act requires the identification of these children whose welfare may be at risk, including children with disabilities, and the provision of information about services available for them and their families to promote their welfare. The provision of accommodation is seen as being one of those services, and fostering is identified as one means of providing it.

This study suggests that short-term foster care is likely to be a particularly relevant service for these children. A large proportion of the children in the sample under study were in voluntary care, and though children were not, prior to the Children Act, identified as being "in need", nonetheless the majority of these children were growing up in situations of difficulty and disharmony and well over half of them were judged to have suffered abuse or neglect at some time in their lives.

Short-term foster care is also needed for children requiring care and protection under court orders and whilst long-term plans are being made and implemented. In Parts IV and V, the Children Act 1989 makes it clear that parental responsibility can only be acquired by a local authority by means of a legal order and requires planning for the continued involvement of parents and others with parental responsibility where this is in the child's best interests. Of the new duties and powers in relation to "looked after" children, the duty to consult and take into account the wishes and feelings of parents and children is very important. Even where compulsion is necessary, the Act places a premium on working in partnership with families,[35] which includes any person with parental responsibility for the child and any person with whom the child has been living, and so is not confined to relatives. This again demands an "inclusive" rather than an "exclusive" model of substitute care provision. How far this can be a reality in relation to short-term foster care, and how levels of agreement and conflict are related to the outcome of the placements is investigated in this study. It also looks at the role of fathers in relation to "looked after" children.

Understanding short-term foster care – theoretical and historical considerations

A discussion of those issues which form a backdrop to present day policy and practice is included in Chapters 1 to 4, which draw together the theoretical and historical knowledge relevant to short-term fostering, and gather, perhaps for the first time, a quantity of detail from the research findings, legislation, theories and models relating to temporary substitute family care.

It has been impossible to include an exhaustive account of all the relevant issues; time and space have precluded the consideration of a number of important themes that are undoubtedly relevant to the provision of short-term fostering. The perspective that is reflected is overwhelmingly white European and American, because that is what has been documented and what is available. The historical experience and theoretical understanding of people from different cultural backgrounds could well form the basis of another study.

Three themes that are crucial in an examination of short-term foster care were identified by Kufeldt in her article on temporary foster care,[36] and are dealt with implicitly throughout the four theoretical chapters. The first theme is the nature of the separation experience itself; the second is the nature and level of involvement of birth parents; and the third concerns the role and function of the foster carer. Knowledge and thinking about each of these themes develops and changes over time, and very much affects the role that short-term foster care has played and could play in child care practice. The way that short-term foster care is provided in the future will continue to be greatly affected by beliefs and positions in relation to these three themes.

The form and content of the book

The book comprises two distinct parts: the theoretical component and the empirical research study. Chapter 1, "Short-term foster care in its child care context", begins by setting short-term foster care in its wider child care context. This is of particular relevance, since short-term foster care is no longer a peripheral activity, but has moved to centre stage in the provision of child care services. In the history of child care, short-term fostering is a relatively recent development, and only emerged in any significant way in the 1950s. Chapter 2, "Short-term fostering – the historical context", examines how it has emerged, and then considers the ways in which subsequent child care legislation and policy have moulded its development as a service, and considers how its popularity has waxed and waned, and its orientation shifted and altered depending on the needs of child care policy. Chapter 3, "From permanency planning to partnership", continues this examination up to the present day and the demands of the Children Act 1989.

Since Bowlby's pioneering work in 1951[37] the crucial significance of theories of attachment and separation in relation to the provision of parenting, and in particular to the provision of substitute parenting, has not been disputed. The analysis, interpretation, and evaluation of the various research findings has provoked much debate and discussion. Chapter 4, "Attachment and separation", examines the current state of knowledge about theories of attachment and separation and considers their relevance for the provision of short-term fostering.

Chapter 5, "The empirical study – overall patterns" and Chapter 6, "Characteristics of the children, their families, and the social work intervention", present the findings of the empirical study. This local study examined 183 placements in short-term foster homes made in a twelve month period in 1988-9 in a local authority social services department.

It is essentially practitioner research as the local authority was the City of Newcastle upon Tyne, where I was then employed. The area covered by Newcastle upon Tyne Social Services includes a large city area in the centre, west and east, with a small suburban area to the north. It was divided at the time of the study into five Area Teams; all five are represented in the study, though some used short-term foster care more than others. The differences and similarities in the catchment areas of the Area Teams provides interesting contrasts and comparisons. Newcastle has always had a higher than average rate of children in care, though as elsewhere, numbers have been falling. From a total of 1,241 children (16.6 per 1000 population) in 1978, it had fallen to 551 (approx 9.0 per 1000 population) in 1988, compared to a national average of 5.9 per 1000 population. In Newcastle in 1988, 67 per cent of the children in care were "boarded out", demonstrating a commitment to this form of child care.[38]

Details of the aims and the methodology used, are also included. Information was gathered from records and by questionnaire, with the aim of describing patterns of use of short-term foster care. The analysis of the data identified the broad characteristics of the placements, and also compared and contrasted placements which were genuinely short (up to three months), with those lasting much longer. The analysis aimed to identify any differences in those children experiencing short placements from those staying longer in "short-term" foster care. Chapter 7, "Conclusions and implications for policy and practice", suggests a model for the provision of short-term foster care in the future, draws together the conclusions from the study, and considers some implications for policy and practice in the light of the requirements of the Children Act 1989.

References

1   Rowe J, Hundleby M, and Garnett L, *Child Care Now*, BAAF, 1989.

2   Triseliotis J, 'Foster care outcomes: a review of key research findings', *Adoption & Fostering*, 13:3, 1989.

3   Berridge D, and Cleaver H, *Foster Home Breakdown*, Blackwell, 1987.

4   Millham S, Bullock R, Hosie K, and Haak M, *Lost in Care: The problems of maintaining links between children in care and their families*, Gower, 1986.

5   Department of Health and Social Security, *Social Work Decisions in Child Care*, HMSO, 1985.

6   Thorpe D, 'Career Patterns in Child Care – Implications for Service', *British Journal of Social Work*, 18:2, 1987.

7   Vernon J, and Fruin D, *In Care: A study of social work decision making*, National Children's Bureau, 1986.

8   See 1 above.

9   See 4 above.

10 Parker R A, *Decision in Child Care*, Allen & Unwin, 1966.

11 George V, *Foster Care: Theory and Practice*, Routledge and Kegan Paul, 1970.

12 Bowlby J, *Child Care and the Growth of Love*, (1st and 2nd edns) Penguin Books, 1953, 1965.

13 See 5 above.

14 Department of Health and Social Security, *Review of Child Care Law*, HMSO, 1985.

15 See 5 above.

16 Department of Health, *The Care of Children: Principles and practice in regulations and guidance*, HMSO, 1989. (See Principle no. 5).

17 Aldgate J, 'Respite care for children – an old remedy in a new package', in Marsh P, and Triseliotis J (eds), *Prevention and Reunification*, Batsford/ BAAF, 1993.

18 See 1 above.

19 See 3 above.

20 See 1 above.

21 See 3 above.

22 See 3 above.

23 See 1 above.

24 See 4 above.

25 See 3 above.

26 See 1 above.

27 Thorpe D, and Bilson A, 'The leaving care curve', *Community Care*, 22 October 1987.

28 See 16 above.

29 Department of Health, *The Children Act 1989 Guidance and Regulations, Volume 3, Family placements*, HMSO, 1991.

30 Department of Health, *Patterns and Outcomes in Child Placement: Messages from current research and their implications*, HMSO, 1991.

31 Hammond C, 'BAAF and the placement needs of children from minority ethnic groups', *Adoption & Fostering*, 14:1, 1990.

32 Triseliotis J (ed), *New Developments in Foster Care and Adoption*, Routledge and Kegan Paul, 1980. (See Chapter 2 for a discussion of inclusive and exclusive models of foster care.)

33 See 31 above.

34 Smith P M, and Berridge D, *Ethnicity and Childcare Placements*, National Children's Bureau, 1993.

35 Department of Health, *The Challenge of Partnership*, HMSO, 1995.

36 Kufeldt K, 'Temporary foster care', *British Journal of Social Work*, 9:1, 1979.

37 Bowlby J, *Maternal Care and Mental Health*, World Health Organisation, 1951.

38 City of Newcastle upon Tyne Social Services, *Report on the Review of Child Care Residential Resources*, 1989.

1 Short-term foster care in its child care context

This chapter examines the research context of the present study and highlights the importance of this form of child care intervention. It considers the significance of the early weeks of care; what is known about the care "experience"; and the characteristics of children in care, including black and minority ethnic children. In short, it examines the wider child care scene in which this in-depth local study is located.

It is difficult to achieve a consensus about what is meant by "short-term" foster care. Berridge and Cleaver[1] defined short-term fostering according to the Boarding Out Regulations 1955, in force at the time of their study in the early 1980s, as placements of up to eight weeks. New boarding out regulations introduced in 1988, and the later Foster Placement (Children) Regulations 1991, no longer make the eight week distinction indicating a move away from simplistic distinctions based on arbitrary time limits towards providing a more differentiated foster care service which carefully matches a child's needs to a range of available resources.

In 1990 Triseliotis[2] defined short-term foster care as 'usually ranging from a few days to about three months', but with the proviso that it sometimes overlaps with intermediate fostering which he defined as 'lasting for an average of two years but a longer period is not ruled out.' He thus acknowledged that short-term fostering had become an umbrella term for a range of fostering activities. Berridge and Cleaver,[3] however, preferred to differentiate short-term from intermediate fostering, suggesting that intermediate fosterings are planned as medium term in duration, are contract based, and task centred. The situation is now complicated further by the fact that in the Guidance and Regulations (Volume 3) attached to the Children Act 1989, "short-term" is used to refer to 'a series of short-term placements of a child with the same foster parent' where certain specific conditions are satisfied; these placements have been more commonly referred to as "respite care".

An important form of child care intervention

There is no doubt, however, that short-term foster care is becoming recognised as an important form of child care intervention. In their study published in 1986, Millham et al[4] were instrumental in identifying the short-term nature of many foster placements. They found that one child in every three entering care was first placed in a short-term foster placement, and 70 per cent of these were discharged home in a matter of weeks once family problems were resolved. Then in 1989 *Child Care Now*[5] confirmed the trend towards shorter episodes in care, reporting a more rapid turnover of care cases. The heavy emphasis on the reduction in the *numbers* of children in care had tended to mask the reality that *admissions* had not declined at the same rate. Indeed, about half of the placements were identified as temporary/emergency foster care, one third as task-centred, and only 10 per cent as long term. Triseliotis[6] summarised the existing research on foster care outcomes in 1989 and noted that short-term fostering affected well over two-fifths of children placed in foster care each year.

Short-term fostering has largely seemed to be a "successful" area of child care, although the measures by which success is judged vary. Berridge and Cleaver[7] concluded from their study of fostering breakdown that 'short-term fostering is an area of child care practice that works reasonably effectively.' Generally they found a very low breakdown rate (only 10 per cent of placements broke down in the eight week period). In total 19 per cent of planned short-term placements broke down. As well as having a relatively low breakdown rate, Berridge and Cleaver also reported that social workers were satisfied with three-quarters of short-term fosterings, had mixed feelings about a fifth, and were seriously concerned about the quality of only four per cent of placements. However, it has already been noted in the Introduction that a number of placements lasted considerably longer than planned and that this in itself constitutes a form of breakdown.

In the same study, Berridge and Cleaver also noted that there were interesting initiatives developing in short-term foster care as an alternative to the more traditional emergency model. They came across a number of examples, including the imaginative provision – sometimes on a structured basis – of respite care for families, and short-term foster homes being used as a base for the assessment of children's needs and problems.

The significance of the early weeks in care

Many of the research studies alluded to above have looked at how long children stay in the care system and the patterns in the rates at which they leave. These studies clearly pointed to the significance of the early weeks in care, and identified a "leaving care curve", a graphic device which illustrated the length of time children spent in the care system and conveyed a simple message: the chances of a child staying in the care system for at least one year almost doubled if he or she had not returned home within six weeks of entering care. The pattern of the curve showed that between a third and a half of the children left within six weeks. For them, care was a relatively brief experience, though a proportion re-entered for a short period or periods within the following year. Beyond two months the "leaving care curve" flattens abruptly – the rate at which children left care diminished and one-third remained in care for a full 52 weeks.

These findings, summarised by Thorpe and Bilson in 1987,[8] were confirmed in 1989 by the *Child Care Now* study which found 46 per cent of the children had left care in two months, 15 per cent left between two and six months, six per cent between six and twelve months, and just two per cent between 12 months and two years. This corroborated the finding that children who do not leave the care system quickly may well remain a very long time.

Millham et al[9] pointed out that this simple pattern – whereby children either leave care very quickly or remain for a much longer period – did not seem to be a logical reflection of the variety and complexity of the presenting problems of children and families. The wide range of children's and families' circumstances would suggest that the leaving patterns of children should be more evenly spread over time. Yet only 14 per cent of their cohort left care in the period between four and twelve months after entering. Their study suggested the pattern occurred because social workers tended to define the task in a way that categorised cases into those that could be dealt with swiftly and those that required much longer intervention, perhaps lasting several years, with few situations falling between these two extremes. The researchers discovered that social workers did have very clear ideas on children's expected length of stay in care, and these estimates proved to be very accurate. They concluded that short-stay children differed significantly from long-stay cases mainly in social workers' expectations of their length of stay.

Certain of the problems which precipitated the admission of children into care could be resolved more quickly than others. Children leaving care quickly were more typically children in voluntary care and straightforward cases of temporary breakdown in family care.[10] Berridge and Cleaver[11] also found that short-term placements were experienced mostly by younger children admitted temporarily to local authority care owing to situational problems, such as illness of parents or housing problems. The average age of the children placed short-term was barely three years, and 70 per cent of them were in voluntary care.

Important distinctions between the different effects of long and short-term placements have been identified. Long stays in care can carry additional hazards: loss of contact with families and frequent placement change;[12] and long-stay children face all the "secondary" problems of being in care, such as distress, affective deprivation, placement breakdowns, and diminished academic achievement, with the added risk of isolation and institutionalisation.[13] However, it has also been shown that short admissions to care can be perceived as helpful.[14]

When Bowlby[15] developed his theories of maternal deprivation, which are discussed in detail in Chapter 4, he linked the interference with early bonds between a mother and child to problems in subsequent development, and this led social workers to be concerned to avoid any type of separation experience. The result was that any type of substitute family care was considered very much a "last resort", only to be used when all else had failed. In consequence, a preponderance of unplanned, emergency admissions, which are more traumatic for the children, occurred.[16] In their study, Rowe et al[17] found 74 per cent of admissions were described as emergencies, in spite of the fact that the overwhelming majority of the children and families (three-quarters) were already known to social services, with 29 per cent having been in care previously.

Millham et al[18] noted that even if a stay in care was short, absence could create serious problems of re-adjustment on return. Chapter 4 looks at findings that suggest that the manner in which children are prepared for leaving and returning home may be as important as the separation itself. Additionally, short-term placement could be a positive, supportive experience if properly planned and prepared for, and if arrangements are made to maintain contact and continuity, and take into account the wider social networks of the child in care, including fathers, wider family and neighbourhood networks.

The care experience

That children can have very different experiences of the care system, depending on their length of stay and the reason for the care episode, was suggested by two separate studies in the mid 1980s. In 1986 Packman et al in Bristol[19] and Vernon and Fruin at the National Children's Bureau[20] suggested that there are in fact three distinct forms of public child care on offer.

The National Children's Bureau suggested that the first involved 'families who are beset by difficulties or handicaps which interrupt or interfere with their capacity to look after their children.'[21] Parents were viewed as unfortunate rather than blameworthy. The second form of care they identified was 'a protection and rescue service for children thought to be in danger, whether it be physical, sexual, moral, emotional and developmental.'[22] Here the emphasis was on parental faults and failings, and on the child as a victim of inadequate or inappropriate parenting. It could involve taking over parental rights and responsibilities. The child care service offered was protection for very vulnerable children.

The third service related to the child whose own behaviour was causing problems, children whose disruptive, antisocial behaviour spread beyond the family. Packman et al[23] termed the three groups respectively, "volunteered", "victims" and "villains", and noted that, in spite of the intentions of the Children and Young Persons Act 1969, the third service was 'as much a retributive and protective service for the public as it is a care service for the young people themselves.'

In addition, Packman et al[24] showed that in their study the sharp distinctions between "admitted" and "not admitted" status were false.

The fact that three out of five children in placement returned home in a very short time demonstrated that the public care system was permeable. Contrary to popular myth, they found that "care" could be a part of the lives of children who for the most part remained with their families. This challenged the notion of a state of "parentlessness" on the part of the child in temporary care, and emphasised the need for children to clearly remain "the children of their own parents".[25] This principle was integrated into the concept of "accommodation" in the Children Act 1989, which can be offered to children in need while their parents retain full "parental responsibility".

The use of compulsory powers was shown to result in interventions being experienced as unhelpful. This was one of the key findings of a number of studies undertaken in the early 1980s and summarised in *Social Work Decisions in Child Care* in 1985.[26] The studies clearly demonstrated the drawbacks of using compulsion in effecting entry to the care system. It had been assumed that acquiring greater legal control would achieve increased stability for a child. The research did not back this up, and found that where children were admitted on a compulsory order they and their families were less likely to find the intervention helpful.

The characteristics of children in placement

As well as differences in the experience of care for long-stay and short-stay children, variations have also been identified in their characteristics, by comparing statistics relating to children admitted to care in a twelve month period, with those relating to children in care at any one point in time (usually the end of the financial year, 31 March). Millham et al[27] found, for example, that 68 per cent of the former were in voluntary care in 1982, compared to only 24 per cent of the latter. They concluded that the juxtaposition of a rapidly changing population of short-term cases alongside a core of children who remained in care made it difficult to generalise about the characteristics of children in care, and suggested that the majority of children who stayed long in the care system were older children and adolescents. End of year figures have tended to emphasise disproportionately older children in long-term care. Figures from the study *Child Care Now*[28] demonstrated more clearly the turnover of children in care, showing that more than half of all admissions were of children under eleven years old, with more than a third being under five; around 12 per cent were of infants under one year old.

Nonetheless there appear to be common factors among all types of children who enter the care system and the most significant is deprivation. Bebbington and Miles[29] investigated in 1987 the family backgrounds of 2,500 children admitted to care in England, in order to quantify the association between indicators of material and social deprivation and entry to care, and to make comparisons with Packman's national survey undertaken in 1962. They found that deprivation was a common factor among all types of children who entered care, and suggested that entry into care was even more closely associated with "deprived" families in their study than it was in 1962. Of their sample, only one quarter were living with both parents; almost three-quarters were from families receiving income support; only one in five lived in owner-occupied housing; and over half were living in poor neighbourhoods. Living with one adult was apparently the greatest single risk factor, with children of mixed race being especially vulnerable to reception into care.

In 1987 Bebbington and Miles[30] observed that there was a far higher proportion of children being admitted primarily for behaviour problems and offences than in 1962. A greater number of older children were entering the care system, and the proportion aged under five on admission had fallen from 56 per cent in 1962 to 30 per cent in 1987, while those aged over 14 had increased from three per cent to 25 per cent. They showed that children can enter care at any age, but the two age groups which were particularly vulnerable were children under one (11 per cent), and those aged 14–15 (23 per cent). The lowest rate of entry occurred between the ages of five and twelve, and some 38 per cent came into care in a family group (with at least one sibling). However, the factor most highly correlated with admission to care changed from "unemployment" in 1962 to "broken family" in 1987.

This is quite consistent with other research studies undertaken in the 1980s. According to Berridge and Cleaver,[31] breakdown in family care accounted for 69 per cent of admissions while the behaviour of the child was the cause of only 25 per cent. They also noted that neglect or abuse affected nearly half their total study group. Millham et al found there was usually a history of disruption and separation among families; entry into care was only one episode in a recurrent and turbulent life cycle. They too noted the family focus of many admissions, with 63 per cent of children being in voluntary care:

> 'It is also clear that many children who come into care will have experienced severe family dislocations. Their family structures are fragile with frequent marital conflicts, cohabitations, and changes of accommodation. Many are families in which there have been significant and recent changes brought about by divorce, separation and cohabitation.'[32]

A number of studies have described how the process of breakdown occurs. In their study of how children enter and leave the care system, Fisher et al[33] described in 1986 how a series of stresses can build up so that the "last straw" can appear to be quite a minor event. Millham et al found a similar pattern: 'While mothers can cope with several disadvantages such as ill-health, poor accommodation and family tensions, a series of crises in rapid succession, which are usually interrelated, put children at risk of separation from their parents.'[34]

Thorpe and Bilson[35] summarised the findings of Packman and Millham and suggested that for many children, including those who had received preventive help, care became unavoidable when because of poverty, ill health and isolation, the resources of many of their families were insufficient to cope with crises caused by sudden illness, relationship breakdown or adolescent difficulties and problems. Rapid change was a feature of these families; family situations not only rapidly deteriorated but also improved. Thorpe and Bilson believed that it was these characteristics of families that resulted in children moving in and out of the care system. They judged that it was impossible to avoid all reactive decision making, because it arose not from the absence of or ill thought out planning and reviewing, but from the unpredictable nature of the predicament of families from which children enter the care system.

This is another argument for rejecting the "last resort" philosophy in relation to short-term admissions. One solution to the problem of drift may have been not to admit children to care. However, if we accept that providing accommodation or care may be necessary and cannot always be controlled (indeed, may also be initiated in crisis by the police, courts or hearings), another solution may be to ensure that a comprehensive set of social work practices and procedures is implemented, designed to restore children quickly to their parents. Under the Children Act 1989 it should now be acceptable to use short-term care as a means of preventing long-term family breakdown.

Black and minority ethnic children and short-term care

There is particular concern, however, about social services provision in relation to black children and families especially for children in the care system who cannot remain with their own families. It is now crucially important to give due attention to issues of race, ethnicity and culture. Legal, professional and moral codes make quite clear the duty 'to ensure that black children and their families receive appropriate and equal services.'[36]

This position, made clear in the Children Act 1989 and accompanying Regulations and Guidance, was reinforced in a letter issued by the Chief Inspector of the Social Services Inspectorate in January 1990 (CI (90) 2) to Directors of Social Services Departments highlighting issues of race and culture in the family placement of children:

> *'Social services must address and seek to meet the needs of children and families from all groups in the community. Society is made up of people of many different ethnic and racial origins and of different religious affiliations. The provision of services which will reach all members of the community calls for the development within social services departments of awareness, sensitivity, and understanding of the different cultures of groups in the local community, and an understanding of the effects of racial discrimination on these groups.'[37]*

A key question is whether foster placements are being used appropriately for black children. Two concerns predominate: firstly, that black children should not be accommodated because of a lack of preventive services suitable to the needs and customs of different ethnic groups; and secondly, that black children should not be denied access to suitable placements because service provision has been developed to meet the needs of the dominant white culture.

Research studies have confirmed that black children were disproportionately represented in admissions to care. They noted the overrepresentation of African and African-Caribbean children in some age
groups in care, and the under-representation of Asian children generally
in the child care statistics.[38] The clearest picture that emerged was that
black children of mixed parentage were grossly over-represented, and
most likely to return to further episodes in care. Bebbington and Miles[39]
found that children of mixed parentage were two and a half times as likely
to enter care, particularly among preschoolers.

A number of suggestions have been proposed to explain why this is
the case. One is that the large numbers of black children in the care system
reflect the disproportionate degrees of poverty and deprivation to which
black people are subjected, and the extent to which families need help.
Black families are potentially significant users of welfare services because
of the social, economic and cultural disadvantages confronting them:
poor housing, high levels of unemployment, inadequate social security
benefits can all result in financial hardship and breakdown of family
relationships.[40] In 1982 Juliet Cheetham[41] explained the over-representa-
tion of black children in the care system thus:

> 'Racial discrimination which denies black families adequate jobs,
> income and housing is the chief cause. This is one reason why
> family breakup and separation of parent and child is much higher
> in the black community in Britain than in the white, and why so
> many black children are taken into care. Another reason for the
> disproportionate numbers of black and mixed race children needing
> new families in Britain is the prejudice and discrimination which
> single white mothers face in caring for mixed race children; this,
> combined with minimal levels of state support for one parent
> families, means that many single mothers have to give up their
> children.'

Alternatively, black families may use the care system as a replacement
for an extended family.[42] A study in the London Borough of Lambeth
found that black families had fewer relatives they could turn to in a family
crisis. It has also been noted that white social workers can fail to
understand and perceive the strengths of black families and that

Eurocentric views about ideal patterns of family life concerning discipline, material and parental responsibilities could exacerbate the risk of reception into care and reduce the chance of return to the parental home.[43]

Where black children are under-represented in the care system questions must be raised as to what is involved in identifying and meeting the needs of children from minority ethnic groups, whether specialist provision for black children is required and desirable, and whether services which tend to be based on white cultural assumptions are accessible or appropriate.

A second key question is whether children must always be placed with families of the same racial background. The issue of transracial placement – the placement of black children in white families – has raised extensive and heated debate, mostly in relation to long-term fostering and adoption. The concerns are equally relevant, though, to short-term placements.

In the 1960s, black children were considered to be "hard to place" together with those who were "handicapped" and "disturbed", and in the main remained in institutions. The pressure in the 1970s to place children out of residential care resulted in the transracial adoption of black children by white families becoming established practice, and foster and adoptive families for black children were almost all white.

Transracial placements have been criticised for being "colour blind": failing to perceive the different needs of black and minority ethnic children, and to recognise the implications of different cultural traditions. They are less able to assist black children in combatting and coping with racism. One of the most significant but equally most controversial criticisms is that transracial placements actually increase racial identity difficulties – where black children grow up experiencing difficulty in maintaining a positive sense of racial identity. An overview of the research from the 1940s by David Milner in 1983, *Children and race: Ten years on*, examines studies which have shown black children to reject their own ethnic or "racial" group by demonstrating a preference for white groups – a form of self rejection – though the view that all black children will have difficulty with ethnic identity has been rejected. Banks suggests way in which social workers and carers can better understand and meet the identity needs of black children.[44]

All black children living away from their own families for any period of time need to be encouraged to develop a positive identity built on an inner core of pride and positive feeling, and to learn how to develop and maintain their self-esteem, identity, and self-respect in a racist society. It is for this reason that the legislation, government guidance and directions, and the major national child care voluntary agencies are unanimous that the placement of choice for a black child is always a black family.[45] Hammond,[46] considering the placement needs of children from minority ethnic groups, summarised the advantages of placing black children in black families thus:

'Black families can offer children an added dimension over and above a loving environment, covering such things as continuity of experience, contact with the relevant community, understanding of and pride in the child's particular inheritance, and skills and support in dealing with racism.'

The Soul Kids Project (1975-6) was the first recruitment campaign targeted specifically at black people. It was a one-year campaign aimed at African-Caribbeans in London. It had the dual aim of publicising the need for foster and adoptive parents and educating both the black community and the social workers about each others' attitudes. In the process, much was learned about the difficulties white workers have in knowing how best to approach prospective black foster carers. The campaign resulted in a much higher number of enquiries from African-Caribbean families and it was recognised that more community work skills were needed in finding families and mobilising community supports and resources.

Nonetheless at present the pool of families available and the complexity and diversity of individual children's child care histories and ethnic origins can make the reality of providing ethnically matched placements within a reasonable time scale very difficult. It must be recognised that not all black children will go to black families. When they do not, their white substitute parents need special preparation and support. John Small has outlined the essential ingredients of any substitute home for black children, and has provided guidelines for the selection and preparation of transracial foster carers.[47] Guidelines on reviewing the placements of black children have been developed by Bradford Social Services Department[48] and could be used alongside the requirements of the Children Act.

Expectations and models of fostering for families from minority ethnic groups may stem from the different types and aims of fostering in different cultures. Ideas, feelings, and assumptions will be based on experience within cultural groups and knowledge of the forms of care available for children. In West Africa, for example, the purpose of fostering is the training or education of the child rather than the provision of substitute parents, and foster parents are expected to be strict with their charges. The fostering relationship does not replace that between birth parents and children, but is experienced as something different and additional to it.[49]

In the Caribbean countries, the birth parents and those providing what we would call "substitute care" for their children will have known each other a long time. The relationship between the birth parents and the caretakers is a non-formal personal one. No great emphasis is placed on the reasons why a child is cared for by someone other than his or her parents, because it is taken for granted that the child can move easily between the households of the extended family and close friends of the family. This means that arrangements for substitute care in Britain may seem unnatural and unfeeling. For example, in the Caribbean, children are not placed with strangers who previously knew nothing about them and their families, and arrangements for visiting birth parents and other relatives are taken for granted; nor does the state play the role of intermediary.[50]

Adoption and fostering as such are concepts that appear to have no direct equivalent in south-east Asian society. The general experience among families of Asian origin is that children who cannot live with their own parents are cared for by the extended family. Where this is not possible the children may be totally rejected.[51] Few children from the Asian communities are received into care and it is likely that white social workers lack understanding of how to support family patterns in these communities.

The Children Act 1989 is the first piece of legislation to address these issues by broadening the ways in which local authorities can provide accommodation to include placements with wider family and friends. It will be important to learn whether there have indeed been significant changes in the provision of family placements for children from minority ethnic communities, and whether new and innovative services develop to meet particular need. If so, it may be an important step in diversifying fostering services for all children.

References

1 Berridge D, and Cleaver H, *Foster Home Breakdown*, Blackwell, 1987.

2 Triseliotis J, *Foster Care Outcomes*, NCB Highlight, No.96, 1990.

3 See 1 above.

4 Millham S, Bullock R, Hosie K, and Haak M, *Lost in Care: The problems of maintaining links between children in care and their families*, Gower, 1986.

5 Rowe J, Hundleby M, and Garnett L, *Child Care Now*, BAAF, 1989.

6 Triseliotis J, 'Foster care outcomes: a review of key research findings', *Adoption & Fostering*, 13:3, 1989.

7 See 1 above.

8 Thorpe D, and Bilson A, 'The leaving care curve', *Community Care*, 22 October 1987.

9 See 4 above.

10 See 4 above.

11 See 1 above.

12 See 8 above.

13 See 4 above.

14 Packman J, Randall J, and Jacques N, *Who Needs Care? Social Work Decisions about Children*, Blackwell, 1986.

15 Bowlby J, *Maternal Care and Mental Health*, World Health Organisation, 1951.

16 See 4 above.

17 See 5 above.

18 See 4 above.

19 See 14 above.

20 Vernon J, and Fruin D, *In Care: A Study of Social Work Decision Making*, National Children's Bureau, 1986.

21 See 20 above.

22 See 20 above.

23 See 14 above.

24 See 14 above.

25 Kufeldt K, 'Temporary foster care', *British Journal of Social Work*, 9:1, 1979.

26 Department of Health & Social Security, *Social Work Decisions in Child Care*, HMSO, 1985.

27 See 4 above.

28 See 5 above.

29 Bebbington A, and Miles J, 'The background of children who enter local authority care', *British Journal of Social Work*, 19:5, 1989.

30 See 29 above.

31 See 1 above.

32 See 4 above.

33 Fisher M, Marsh P, and Phillips D with Sainsbury E, *In and Out of Care*, Batsford/BAAF, 1986.

34 See 4 above.

35 See 8 above.

36 Macdonald S, *All Equal under the Act*, (REU) Personal Social Services, 1991. Macdonald defines the term "black" as denoting people from specific ethnic minority groups who suffer racism because of their skin colour.

37 Social Services Inspectorate, 'Issues of race and culture in the family placement of children', Letter to Directors of Social Services, CI(90)2, Department of Health, 1990.

38 A comprehensive summary of the research is included in Department of Health, *Patterns and Outcomes in Child Placement: Messages from current research and their implications*, HMSO, 1991.

39 See 29 above.

40 Bradshaw J, *Child Poverty and Deprivation in the UK*, National Children's Bureau, 1990.

41 Cheetham J (ed), *Social Work & Ethnicity*, Allen & Unwin, 1982.

42 See 5 above.

43 Ahmed S, Cheetham J, and Small J, *Social Work with Black Children and their Families*, Batsford/BAAF, 1986. The introduction to this book contains a very comprehensive review of the literature and consideration of these issues.

44 Banks N, 'Techniques for direct identity work with black children', *Adoption & Fostering*, 16:3, 1992.

45 Smith P M, and Berridge D, *Ethnicity and Childcare Placements*, National Children's Bureau, 1993.

46 Hammond C, 'BAAF and the placement needs of children from minority ethnic groups', *Adoption & Fostering*, 14:1, 1990.

47 See 43 above.

48 See 43 above.

49 Holman R, *Trading in Children*, Routledge & Kegan Paul, 1973.

50 See 41 above.

51 Cann W, 'Meeting the needs of the Asian community', *Adoption & Fostering*, 8:1, 1984.

2 Short-term fostering – the historical context

Fostering as we know it today developed in the latter part of the last century, an offshoot of the philanthropic movement of that period. Its aim was to provide a more beneficial alternative to the workhouse or district school for 'small numbers of orphan and totally deserted children'.[1] Short-term fostering was, however, a much later development. This chapter discusses its emergence in the 1950s, when Bowlby, in particular, advocated the use of foster care for the short-stay placements of young children, having examined the psychological effects of "maternal deprivation" and highlighted the deficiencies of institutional care in providing for the proper development of young children.[2]

The development of the use of fostering for short-term placements was part of the reason for the expansion of boarding out in the decade that followed.[3] In spite of this, however, professional and research interest focused on the more problematic aspects of fostering. Firstly, concern was expressed about the high rate of fostering breakdown and its harmful effects on the child's emotional development.[4,5,6] Later, in the early part of the 1970s, the need to find permanent placements for thousands of children – some considered "hard-to-place" for reasons of age, disability, race and behavioural difficulties, yet identified as needing permanent substitute families – took precedence.[7] Providing children with permanence and stability outside their own homes (if it could not be found within them) became a priority task.[8] Only in the mid-1980s has research and interest begun to focus on short-term fostering, and its value and significance recognised.[9,10]

This chapter traces the developments in the early use of fostering which have influenced our understanding of the role of short-term fostering and examines why it has taken so long for it to be recognised as an important and distinctive form of child care provision.

Fostering as quasi-adoption – the "fresh start" view

In earlier days there was no possibility that a fostering arrangement could be considered temporary or impermanent. Prior to the Children Act 1948, the largest group of children requiring care away from their own homes were those maintained by local authorities under the Poor Law Acts as poor persons in need of relief.[11] The Poor Law Board Report of 1869 stressed that 'it is most important on all grounds to avoid severing or weakening in any way the ties of family, even where owing to the character of the parents, it might be thought that the children could be benefitted by removal from their control.'[12] Consequently fostering was seen as a form of quasi-adoption, and only suitable for those children for whom there was no possibility at any stage of a return home.

From 1870 until as late as 1945 boarding out of these "Poor Law" children was restricted by various Public Assistance Orders. First, it was restricted specifically to orphans and deserted children. Legislation was then passed at the end of the 19th century which authorised that parental rights could be assumed over children whose parents were deemed to have deserted them.[13] Following this, the boarding out restrictions were amended to include children in respect of whom the authorities had assumed parental rights and powers. The Curtis Committee in 1946 identified them as constituting around 16 per cent of the children in care of the Poor Law Authorities.

The early pioneers in foster care believed, and this view held strong until the 1940s, that removing a child from an inadequate home background and placing him or her in a foster home would enable the child to forget past experiences and start afresh – the "fresh start" view. The aim was to rescue children and give them the benefit of the experiences of family life away from the contamination of persons of the "prostitute and loafer type".[14] The positive concept of the foster mother, the ideal, was of a woman motivated by charity. She was expected to take over the role of the natural mother. The arrangement was thought of as permanent, and the complete break with the family of origin was an integral part of the system.[15]

Fostering was a favoured form of care, yet was only used for a minority of deprived children. Reports indicting large residential establishments – notably the Mundella Report of 1896, which examined the standard of health of children brought up in large institutions – recommended that government policy be altered so as 'to encourage and not to hinder the extension of the boarding out system'.[16] In spite of this early recognition of the value of foster care, the proportion of children boarded out in fact decreased in the years between 1900 and 1939. Figures drawn from the annual reports of the Local Government Board (later Ministry of Health) showed that 18.4 per cent were boarded out in 1900 and only 15.7 per cent were boarded out in 1939, this representing a drop in the actual number of children boarded out.[17]

In 1945, restrictions on the use of boarding out were eventually revoked to facilitate the continuance of private care for Poor Law children who had been billeted under the evacuation scheme. Even so, by the end of the war in 1946 the proportion of children boarded out had only risen to 29 per cent.[18] The main reason for this seems to have been a shortage of satisfactory foster homes, and one reason proffered for this was the 'strong dread of becoming attached to a child who may be removed after a year or two from the foster parents' care. Interference by the child's real parents is feared and disliked.'[19]

Not all the boarded out children, however, were the responsibility of the Public Assistance Committees. Some were children committed to the care of "fit persons" under the Children and Young Persons Act 1933. Under the Act, local authorities were empowered to board out children and young persons committed to their care, and the Children and Young Persons (Boarding Out) Rules made boarding out obligatory on the local authority, with the exception of special cases. There was no mention of the eventual return of the child to his or her own family.[20] Additionally, a large proportion of the children who had no homes of their own were cared for by charitable organisations and in "voluntary homes" without ever have been brought before a court or made chargeable to a Poor Law Authority. The kind of experience these children may have had, of living in a variety of fostering and institutional settings, has been well documented in Janet Hitchman's autobiographical novel.[21] Additionally, healthy children under the age of five could be maintained under the Public Health Act 1936, with powers exercised through the Maternity and Child Welfare Committees. Some authorities established residential nurseries for the care of children whose mothers were unable to take charge of them. In a few areas the Act was also used to cover the placing of infants in foster homes by the Public Health Authority (no figures given).

Under the child life protection provisions of the Public Health Act 1936, people "nursing or maintaining" children under nine years for "reward", i.e. private foster children, had to notify the welfare authority. At the end of 1944 there were over 14,000 children under the supervision of welfare authorities in accordance with these provisions.[22] Unfortunately there is little information about these children or the duration of their foster placements.

Although at this time fostering had really only been used for long-stay admissions, there is evidence that the majority of admissions to care were short-stay. In 1946 the Curtis Committee reported the following:

'A striking fact that has emerged from our evidence is the large proportion of Public Assistance admissions which are of the "short-stay" character. The proportion has been put as high as 60 per cent by the National Association of Administrators of Local Government Establishments and this is confirmed by the evidence of the London County Council.'[23]

How were these short-stay children accommodated? At that time children under three were still cared for in nurseries in public assistance institutions, though the establishment of separate nurseries was 'growing with official encouragement'. Children between three and 16 years were only allowed to stay in the workhouse for six weeks, and the authority was empowered to provide for the children by maintaining them in institutions described as "schools", but which were really different types of children's homes.[24]

The Curtis Report advocated the use of reception homes to serve as the "short-stay" homes needed for children whose parents were temporarily unable to look after them, for example, if the mother was having another baby.[25] These homes also provided "places of safety" for children needing care or protection, and as the first refuge for destitute children. This was not because the Committee found institutional care satisfactory, but it was considered better than the status quo in some authorities, where children were left with nothing but the barest provision of physical care 'not only for weeks, but for months'.[26]

There was no mention of boarding out being used for any "short-stay" purposes. Fostering was still largely regarded as 'the best method short of adoption of providing the child with a substitute for his own home'.[27]

A unified service for deprived children – the Children Act 1948

When the recommendations of the Curtis Committee were embodied in the Children Act 1948 a number of changes were incorporated which were to radically change the use of foster care. The provisions of the new Act were designed to ensure that all children in the care of local authorities or voluntary organisations were brought up in good conditions, and in an atmosphere of security and affection comparable with that enjoyed by a child living in his or her own home with good parents.[28] Under the Act, fostering became the placement of first choice where adoption was not possible.

Prior to the passing of the Children Act 1948, central responsibility for the care of children away from their own homes had been divided among several government departments. The Act set up Children's Departments and the new departments' duties relating to children "received" into care were taken over from the Public Assistance Committees, and enshrined in Section 1 of the 1948 Act. This was a service for destitute children and was essentially providing care for the children of parents who requested it. The duties in relation to children "committed" to care were taken over from local education authorities and were under the Children and Young Persons Act 1933, which allowed children in need of care through neglect, cruelty, truanting, moral danger, or committing an offence to be committed to care under Fit Person Orders.

Thus the central responsibility of the new Act was the care of all children "deprived of a normal home life" either temporarily or permanently.[29] The central task of the child care service at its inception was the provision of good substitute care for these deprived children with the duty to board out "wherever suitable homes could be found".[30]

In spite of fostering now being the preferred method of providing substitute care, a further significant change included in the Act was that local authorities were also required to endeavour to return the child to the care of parents, guardians or relatives where it was "consistent with the welfare of the child". This rehabilitative duty changed the role and purpose of fostering and foster parents. Prior to the 1948 Act, fostering was seen as an alternative to parental care and the foster parents took on the birth parents' role. Post 1948 fostering was intended to be more often a short-term or impermanent arrangement with foster parents not seeking to replace the parent to whom the child could eventually return, incorporating a far greater degree of sharing. If children were to be rehabilitated, they were to be kept in close touch with their birth parents.

A further new aim of the Act was to raise the standard of substitute care following concerns raised by the Monckton Inquiry into the death of Dennis O'Neill in his foster home in 1945, and by the Curtis Committee in its report in 1946. The Act was intended to do away with the Poor Law notion of "less eligibility", and authorised optimal provision for children in care rather than minimal. Now when a child was in care, the Children's Departments had to 'further his best interests and afford him opportunity for the proper development of his character and abilities' and 'use such facilities and services available for children in the care of their own parents'.

Following the 1948 Act with the publicity of the new service and the presentation of hitherto unmet needs, the figures for children in care rose to 55,000 in 1949 and to a peak of 65,000 in 1953.[31]

The 1950s – expansion in the use of foster care

The wider use of boarding out was further encouraged early in the 1950s by significant research into child development. Of particular influence was the work of Bowlby for the World Health Organisation. His monograph in 1951 stressed the prime significance of the child's earliest ties to mother and the need for a 'warm, intimate and continuous relationship'.[32] He advocated fostering rather than placement in an institution and stressed the advantages of familiar people to foster. He maintained that children thrived better in bad homes than in good institutions and that a residential nursery could not provide a satisfactory emotional environment for infants and young children. This lent support to the preference for foster care as a placement over children's homes.[33]

It reinforced the concept of fostering as the preferred method of providing substitute care.

In 1950 the proportion of children boarded out was around 37 per cent. By 1955 boarding out had increased considerably and the proportion was now 44 per cent of the children in care. In addition, it was clear that the role and purpose of foster care had already begun to develop. The 7th Report of the Children's Department by the Home Office, published in 1955, commented that it was remarkable how many foster parents were prepared to accept a foster child as a member of their family while recognising the prior claim of the parents to the child's love and loyalty. In 1957 Gray and Parr conducted an inquiry for the Home Office into children in care and the recruitment of foster parents. They found great importance was being attached to the desirability of securing a child's return home to the family circle as soon as possible and that work was being carried out to rehabilitate the family where this was necessary. By the time of their report about half the children in care were boarded out. Interestingly, only 30 per cent of them were with recruited foster parents (as opposed to "de facto" placements).[34]

In 1955 new Boarding Out Regulations were issued by the Home Office, and a new distinction was drawn between short and long-term fostering. In the early 1950s many admissions to care were of short duration. An immense pressure of applications for *temporary* reception into care was one result of the new Act and of the new unified Children's Service.[35] Bowlby's writings published in 1953[36] led to an increase in the use of foster care specifically for these placements. He recommended the use of temporary foster parents for short-term emergency admissions. The child's links with his or her natural family were stressed as was the need to restore the child wherever possible. His work also resulted in the closure of residential nurseries; this created extra demand for foster placements for short-term admissions of young children.

Gray and Parr also found that a considerable number of children who came into care during the course of a year remained in care for only a short time – some only for a few weeks – and they were then able to go home. The two reasons accounting for the largest annual intake were the confinement of the mother and other short-term illness of the parent or guardian, and these reasons accounted for 52.3 per cent of all the children coming into care during the year (ended 31 March 1956). That their stay in care was short is confirmed by the fact that only 5.7 per cent of all the children in care at any one point in time had come into care for these two reasons.[37]

Gray and Parr also note a significant distinction between short-term and long-term foster parents. They reported that some foster parents may have had one child for many years, and would perhaps continue to take an interest after the child had passed out of care and become independent. Others had a succession of foster children for short periods. They also found that in some areas a list was kept of foster parents who were prepared to take children in an emergency at a few hours notice.[38]

Gray and Parr's survey also provided rough estimates of the proportion of the intake at a given point in time which would still be in care at a given later date. After six weeks about 50 per cent would still be in care, 23 per cent after a year, 19 per cent after two years, and 11 per cent would still be in care after five years. The rate at which children left care may, therefore, have remained fairly consistent over time, as these figures are remarkably similar to the pattern more recently depicted in the "leaving care curve" described in Chapter 1.[39]

By the early 1960s the proportion of children boarded out was over 50 per cent, reaching a peak of 52 per cent in 1963.[40] This was attributed by Parker[41] to a number of important and inter-related factors. He cited deficiencies in institutional care; theories of maternal deprivation; the lack of residential accommodation; that fostering was more economical; and notably, that short-term as well as long-term foster care came to be seen as both possible and desirable. This increased its scope considerably.

However, when the 9th Report of the work of the Children's Department (1961-1963) reported these further rises in the percentage of children in care in foster homes, it also recognised, for the first time, that 'boarding out is not necessarily the best thing for every child'. Consequently this was to be for some time the high water mark for fostering.[42] Thereafter, although the actual number of children who were fostered continued to rise slightly for a time, the proportion that they represented of all children in care declined. In 1970 it was 42 per cent.[43]

The 1960s – new approaches to foster care

Research and experience caused social services departments to question their original commitment to fostering. Children placed in foster homes did not always settle happily; some had to be removed because their behaviour became intolerable to the foster parents or because social workers were convinced that their needs were not being met satisfactorily: 'Transplanting a child proved to be as delicate an operation as transplanting any human organ. There was always the risk of rejection.'[44]

The writings of Bowlby had been influential in the abandonment of the "fresh start" view in foster placements. His emphasis on the effects of maternal deprivation on personality development indicated how important it was to know what experiences the child had had in his or her birth family which would affect adjustment in the foster home.[45] He asserted that children 'are not slates from which the past can be rubbed by a duster or sponge, but human beings who carry their previous experiences with them and whose behaviour in the present is profoundly affected by what has gone before'.[46] When Gordon Trasler studied foster placement breakdowns in Devon over a period of three years in the early 1950s, he too concluded that a child's early experiences were a significant factor in the breakdown of foster placements.[47] This study was the first of a number of important studies of fostering breakdown. Trasler suggested an average failure rate of between one-third and two-fifths over all long-term placements.[48] Parker studied all long-term foster placements arranged in Kent in 1952 and 1953, five years after the placements began, and reported a failure rate of 48 per cent.[49] George looked at placements in three authorities between 1961 and 1963 and calculated the failure rate was as high as 59.8 per cent.[50]

During the 1960s fostering lost its leading position. However, the concentration of studies on long-term fostering had tended to exaggerate the extent of failure in that shorter term but successful fosterings, where children had been rehabilitated, were not considered.[51] Parker made it clear that his study was limited to those placements which were of a long-term nature, and recognised the distinctions between long and short-term foster care.

The contribution that short-term foster care was making may also have been discounted at this time because of a new trend which preferred prevention to care in any shape or form. As the awareness grew of the importance of an undisturbed family life to the developing child, the task of how to deal with the problem of 'the adequacy and integrity of a large number of families'[52] became increasingly more urgent. The trend towards increasing use of short-term care was deplored by the Schaffers in their study of short-term admissions in the late 1960s, for they saw the need for short-term foster care as an indicator of weakness in family relationships.[53]

In 1960 the Ingleby Committee had highlighted the link between child neglect and juvenile delinquency, and that there was a need for an optimal level of parental care for children living at home in the community as well. It considered whether local authorities should be given new powers to prevent suffering through neglect in children's own homes. Consequently, while the Children and Young Persons Act 1963 is largely about delinquency and the juvenile court system, preventive work was sanctioned by Section 1 of the Act, and was concerned with decreasing the need to receive children into care or to keep them in care. This considerably altered the balance of work within the child care service. Within a short time children "in care" were vastly outnumbered by children receiving attention in their own homes.

These changes had considerable implications for foster care. The use of foster homes for short-term care had already been increased due to the closure of residential establishments. There was a growing appreciation of the complex dynamics of the inter-relationships between the child, their birth family and the foster family. In 1965 Olive Stevenson recognised that foster care had become 'a highly skilled job which needs more knowledge than ordinary parenthood'.[54] Foster carers were increasingly being asked to see the child as part of his or her birth family, involving direct contact between parent and foster parents, and indeed, as part of the push towards preventative work, foster carers were asked to play a part in the rehabilitation of the family as a whole. Foster care came to be seen more as a temporary measure intended to get the child's family back on its feet again. However, the emphasis on prevention meant that the recruiting and selection of foster homes was no longer a priority, with the result that some foster homes were overused, and the selection of the right foster home for a child would sometimes be Hobson's Choice.

It also altered the type of children coming forward for fostering, as those needing admission were likely to be the ones presenting the most difficult problems. It was accepted that children in care were more maladjusted, with more deep-rooted problems than used to be the case.[55] This was exacerbated by the gradual incorporation of disturbed and delinquent children into the child care service with the Children and Young Persons Act 1969.[56] The Children and Young Persons Acts of 1963 and 1969 widened the scope of the work of Children's Departments. Then in 1970 the Local Authority Social Services Act absorbed them into new social services departments.[57] As a consequence, specialist skills became diluted, and reliance on accumulated practice wisdom was no longer possible.[58]

The reasons why children needed foster care had undoubtedly altered. There was a reduced need for long-term care because few deprived children were actually orphans. The reasons for their being in care were more usually to do with family breakdown which could be temporary. George[59] found that it was clear that boarding out was mainly being used for children whose parents were separated or if one of them had died. Less than one quarter of the children had married parents who were living together at the time of placement.[60] Parker found an equally small proportion (20 per cent) of birth parents living together at the time of placement.[61]

The role the foster mother was required to play had become more akin to that of a temporary caretaker or guardian. Parker reported that with the aim of rehabilitation, and the general expansion of short-term care, children's departments were anxious that the subsequent reunification of the child with his or her family should not be prejudiced by allowing the placement to slip into semi-adoption.[62] In embracing the goals of prevention and rehabilitation, the child care services' expectations of fostering therefore had to develop in the direction of a "professional" service, with foster carers perceived as a species of residential care worker, operating from their own homes. Indeed, George favoured the title "foster care worker" as one way of avoiding the new ambiguities and conflicts in the fostering role created by its emphasis on co-operation between the parties and on rehabilitation of foster children to their birth parents.[63]

The 1960s was also a period of conflict about the nature and desirability of fostering.[64] It witnessed a number of debates concerning the role of the foster carer, the nature and purpose of fostering, and the distinction between short-term and long-term foster care. Adamson found that all departments had different expectations of short-term and long-term foster parents. Most departments were able to build up a fairly satisfactory panel of short-term foster carers who agreed to take a child or children at short notice: a panel of long-term foster carers was more difficult to achieve, partly because of the slow turnover of children, and partly because, as Adamson noted, 'long-term fostering is a different and often more difficult task, and thus fewer candidates are suitable'.[65] She also observed the frequent contact between agency and the short-term foster mothers who worked for a department for a number of years, who did indeed appear to be an extension of the caring staff and understood well the policy of the department with regard to child care.[66]

George's study[67] highlighted differences in theory and practice in relation to the foster carer role, between the image that they were professional workers whose main aim was to help the foster child and their parents, and the fact that half the foster carers' responses in the study were in line with the view that in their role they resembled the foster child's birth parents. George suggested that apart from adoptive parents, there were three groups of foster care workers:

i)   short-term foster care workers who care for children for short periods while a permanent plan is made, eg. move the child into an establishment, place the child with adoptive parents or return the child to his or her parents as soon as the parents recover from their short-term incapacity.

ii) the foster care workers who care for children for long periods, but where the aim is to rehabilitate the child to his or her parents.

iii) the long-term foster care workers for children whose parents are out of the picture completely or whose parents maintain some contact but will not make a home for them.[68]

Adamson[69] suggested that a new approach was needed to foster home care, which viewed temporary care for deprived children as a community service. She identified a great need for temporary care as a "helping" service, and recommended that the service should be made more attractive by offering more realistic payments to enable the foster child to be given equal treatment with the couple's own children. Although it was felt that foster carers might not get the same emotional reward from the fostering task, as they would need to 'keep a detached, controlled, non-possessive attitude towards the foster child', nonetheless Adamson observed:

> 'Many foster parents care successfully for children whose parents continue to keep in contact with them and who are able to have them at home with them for long periods. In fact this is the situation with the majority of children in care. They belong to families which are able to function adequately so long as no particular crisis arises but once something goes wrong, then the unit falls apart. And this is where the foster family steps in to take over some of the problems, one or two of the children, until the children's own parents can cope again.'[70]

In 1975 Holman[71] reviewed a number of contemporary research studies, mainly of long-term fosterings, and identified and described two contrasting concepts of fostering. These were labelled as "inclusive" and "exclusive". What Adamson was describing was an example of an "inclusive" type of fostering. "Inclusive" fostering, Holman suggested, is based on a readiness to draw various components – the birth parents, knowledge of them, and contact with social workers – into the fostering situation with the foster carers and the foster child; birth parents are regarded positively, with a willingness that the children should possess full knowledge about them, and social workers are also included. Most short-term and medium term placements are of this nature. This type of fostering has been shown to facilitate rehabilitation, and can be used successfully for the relief of families under stress, and for the treatment of many child or family problems.

"Exclusive" fostering attempts to contain the child within the foster family while excluding other connections in order to promote security and continuity for the foster child. Opinions of birth parents tend to be hostile. The foster carers do not talk to the foster children about their backgrounds, nor encourage any contact with the birth family for fear the fostering will be disturbed. In addition they are uneasy about receiving social work support.[72]

The 1970s – which way for foster care?

Although agencies increasingly valued the "inclusive" model of foster care, in practice many foster carers still viewed themselves as substitute parents. In 1969 Timms[73] acknowledged the difficulties implicit in sharing the care of a child, and that many foster carers found it hard to tolerate the child's contact with their birth family. He distinguished between 'the policy aims set by one actor in a situation (a children's department) and the actual outcome.'[74]

In 1975 Shaw and Lebens interviewed a sample of foster carers of a group of children expected to grow up in care. They found the foster carers viewed fostering in terms of natural parenthood; they preferred birth parents not to visit; they were, in their own eyes, engaged in the task of bringing up children as they would a child of their own.[75]

Some of the problems in implementing the type of inclusive fostering advocated by Adamson above became apparent. Parker's[76] study had noted, for example, the difficulty of determining just how long a child was likely to be staying in care. Hence many foster placements which clearly began as short-term grew into long-term arrangements, often successfully, but incidentally "blocking" a number of foster carers who had been specifically chosen for short-term cases. Adamson reported a significant difference in the relationships within the foster family after about three years. Goals that were compatible in the short-term – loving care in a substitute family and restoration to the natural family – could become incompatible in the course of time. It was thought that a child's "natural" bonds might weaken as the allegiance to the foster family grew and ultimately rehabilitation became unrealistic. This resulted in the rejection of impermanent fostering of an indeterminate duration.[77]

At the beginning of the 1970s there was a generally held assumption that most foster placements were of intermediate length with the aim of eventual rehabilitation, and the discussion about the foster carers role was based on the expectations that the child would be going back to his or her own family of origin. However, it seemed increasingly that these policies were out of line with realities. The phenomenon of drift was first identified in the USA by Maas and Engler, who described foster children as 'the orphans of the living'.[78] *Children Who Wait*[79] demonstrated that the same problem existed in the UK child care system. It showed that if children did not return home within a few months they were likely to remain in care for a very long time. Rehabilitation to birth parents was frequently difficult to achieve. Some 72 per cent of children needing foster placements were thought to need a permanent home. *Children Who Wait* suggested that in 1971 there were as many as 7,000 children in the care of statutory and voluntary agencies throughout the British Isles who, on their social worker's own admission, needed a substitute family but were still in residential care.

The study by Shaw and Lebens[80] confirmed that 'the break in the so-called "continuum of care" for children comes not at the far end between long-term care and adoption, but much sooner, between short-term foster care and the rest. Whether six months in care is the significant point of no return is unclear – it is certainly no later and may well be months earlier in some cases. What matters most is that for such children life with their families of origin is not seen as a viable option.' The fact was that there were comparatively few medium length fostering placements. Once having entered the care system children tended to remain there and drift.

Debates grew up around the nature of parent–child relationships, bonding and separation, child development and the passage of time. The plight of children who did return to their birth families after lengthy periods in foster care was tragically and poignantly illustrated by the death of Maria Colwell at the hands of her stepfather in 1973. Maria had been happily fostered by her aunt for much of her childhood. When her birth mother remarried Maria returned to live with her. Maria was subjected to physical and emotional abuse and neglect until her death.

The solution to these problems was to legitimise "exclusive" fostering and increase legal security for children such as Maria who had put down roots in a successful foster placement. The 1975 Children Act conferred the benefits of adoption upon a wider range of children and adoption was finally integrated into the mainstream of child care.[81]

At the same time the 1970s saw the rise of "professional" fostering. The professional carers stressed the therapeutic and caretaking aspects of the role, seeing themselves as colleagues of social workers, and expected special training. They were recruited for new specialist fostering schemes for children with physical and mental disabilities, disturbed adolescents, other children with behaviour problems, and children from minority ethnic groups. There had also been an enormous increase in the temporary fostering of children who were in care for a matter of weeks or months in time of family crisis. At the same time that the 1975 Children Act strengthened the position of foster parents and provided them with the opportunity to acquire greater legal security, the official guidance on foster care stressed an "inclusive" model of the fostering process: *Foster Care: A guide to practice* stated in 1976 'The very essence of this process is that his [or her] care is shared and his [or her] parents have a very important part to play.'[82]

Short-term foster care, however, was to wait yet another decade before it began to receive the attention it already deserved. In the meantime child care policy chose another route. From the mid-1970s, permanency planning became a universally accepted way of working with children and families. Short-term foster care was adapted to take on a new role and function in relation to the process of assessing birth families' capacity to provide for children throughout their lifetime, or, if that was not possible, the role of caring for a child until he or she was able to move into a permanent substitute family.

References

1 House of Commons Report 1870, cited in George V, *Foster Care: Theory and practice*, Routledge & Kegan Paul, 1970.

2 Bowlby J, *Child Care and the Growth of Love*, (1st & 2nd edns), Penguin Books, 1953, 1965.

3 Parker R A, *Decision in Child Care*, Allen & Unwin, 1966.

4 Trasler G, *In Place of Parents: A study of foster care*, Routledge & Kegan Paul, 1960.

5 George V, *Foster Care: Theory and practice*, Routledge & Kegan Paul, 1970.

6 See 3 above.

7 Rowe J & Lambert L, *Children who Wait*, ABAFA, 1973.

8 Triseliotis J (ed), *New Developments in Foster Care and Adoption*, Routledge & Kegan Paul, 1980.

9   Rowe J, Hundleby M, and Garnett L, *Child Care Now*, BAAF, 1989.

10 Berridge D, and Cleaver H, *Foster Home Breakdown*, Blackwell, 1987.

11 Home Office, *Report of the Care of Children Committee*, (Curtis Report), Cm 6922, HMSO, 1946.

12 Cited in 5 above.

13 See 5 above.

14 See 5 above.

15 Adamson G, *The Caretakers*, Bookstall Publications, 1972.

16 See 5 above.

17 See 3 above.

18 Packman J, *The Child's Generation*, (2nd edn), Blackwell/Robertson, 1981.

19 See 11 above, Section III.

20 See 11 above, Section I.

21 Hitchman J, *The King of the Barbareens*, Penguin Books, 1960.

22 See 11 above, Section I.

23 See 11 above, Section III.

24 See 11 above, Section I.

25 See 11 above, Section III.

26 See 11 above, Section II.

27 See 15 above.

28 Gray P G, and Parr E A, *Children in Care and the Recruitment of Foster Parents*, COI, The Social Survey, 1957.

29 See 18 above.

30 See 15 above.

31 See 18 above.

32 Bowlby J, *Maternal Care and Mental Health*, World Health Organisation, 1951.

33 Rutter M, *Maternal Deprivation Reassessed*, (1st and 2nd edns) Penguin Books, 1972, 1981.

34 See 28 above.

35 See 18 above.

36 See 2 above.

37 See 28 above.

38 See 28 above.

39 Thorpe D, and Bilson A, 'The leaving care curve', *Community Care*, 22 October, 1987.

40 See 18 above.

41 See 3 above.

42 See 18 above.

43 See 18 above.

44 See 18 above.

45 See 4 and 5 above.

46 See 33 above.

47 See 4 above.

48 See 4 above.

49 See 3 above.

50 See 5 above.

51 Holman R, 'Exclusive and inclusive concepts of fostering', in Triseliotis J (ed), *New Developments in Foster Care and Adoption*, Routledge & Kegan Paul, 1980, is a part-reprint from the *British Journal of Social Work*, 5:1, 1975.

52 Schaffer H R, and Schaffer E B, *Child Care and the Family*, Occasional Papers on Social Administration, No. 25, 1968.

53 See 52 above.

54 Stevenson O, *Someone Else's Child*, Routledge & Kegan Paul, 1965.

55 See 15 above.

56 See 18 above.

57 See 4 above.

58 Rowe J, 'Fostering in the 1970s and beyond', ABAFA. Reprinted in Triseliotis J (ed), *New Developments in Foster Care and Adoption*, Routledge & Kegan Paul, 1980.

59 See 5 above.

60 See 5 above.

61 See 3 above.

62 See 3 above.

63 See 5 above.

64 See 4 above.

65 See 15 above.

66 See 15 above.

67 See 5 above.

68 See 5 above.

69 See 15 above.

70 See 15 above.

71 See 51 above.

72 See 51 above.

73 Timms N, *Casework in the Child Care Service*, (2nd edn) Butterworths, 1969.

74 See 73 above.

75 Shaw M, and Lebens K, 'Children between families', *Adoption & Fostering*, 84:2, 1976.

76 See 3 above.

77 See 18 above.

78 Maas H, and Engler R, *Children in Need of Parents*, Columbia University

Press, 1959, USA.

79 See 7 above.

80 See 75 above.

81 See 18 above.

82 Department of Health & Social Security, *Foster Care: A guide to practice*, HMSO, 1976.

3   From permanency planning to partnership

Amidst the concern to clarify the confusion surrounding the role and function of foster carers, a number of developments on the child care scene resulted, in the 1970s and 1980s, in a radical rethink of child care policy and practice away from total commitment to prevention and rehabilitation. This was to have such considerable effect on the way that short-term foster care was viewed and the roles that it was required to play, that it is worth examining these changes in some detail to fully understand the forces at work in shaping perceptions of short-term care.

This chapter traces the developments in child care philosophy that occurred between the Children Acts of 1975 and 1989, and examines their effects on the British child care scene, and on the role of short-term fostering. The increased complexity in child care policy and practice, including developments in permanency planning, resulted in a number of different strands being woven into the role and function of short-term foster care.

Rethinking policy

A number of worrying themes had emerged in the early part of the 1970s. George's study confirmed that high levels of foster placement breakdown continued.[1] Rowe and Lambert, in *Children Who Wait*[2] had highlighted the problem of "drift" in care and the deficiency in planning for children, and showed that policies of prevention and rehabilitation were not working as people had hoped. An estimated 7,000 children were adrift in residential care needing substitute families. At the same time the tragedy of the death of Maria Colwell,[3] abused and killed by her step-father on her return to the care of her birth mother after spending much of her early childhood in foster care, emphasised other personal costs that might be paid by some children as a consequence of policies that emphasised prevention or rehabilitation as the only goals in child care. The result was a rethink of policy which, occurring at the same time as the Houghton Committee, influenced the Children Act 1975, and paved the way for more assertive planning for children entering the care system.[4]

In 1973 the first of two books by Goldstein, Freud and Solnit,[5] raised the issue of "psychological parenting" and its relation to the whole concept of "permanence". By "psychological parenting" was meant the permanent and exclusive relationship between a child and his or her "parent" (irrespective of blood ties) which was seen as all important for the satisfactory emotional growth and development of a child.

Goldstein, Freud and Solnit made a number of assertions. They believed that being a child's psychological parent was a "dichotomous option" – the adult either was or was not; there were no gradations of psychological parenting. Secondly, a child could have one or two psychological parents, but no more, and was not capable of dealing with situations where they maintained contact with birth parents while living with a set of substitute parents. Thirdly, the child's sense of time so differed from that of an adult that the relationship between a child and his or her psychological parents (be they biological or not) could be broken by even short absences, depending on the age of the child, or by disputes over custody. At the time, these assertions achieved a high degree of acceptance, and gave theoretical credence to the "exclusive" model of substitute care, and to any tendencies of social workers and foster carers to collude to exclude birth parents.

In 1977 James and Joyce Robertson expounded the implications of the notion of "psychological parenting" for foster care:[6]

> *'Whoever loves and looks after a young child in the early years, whether she is the blood mother, adoptive mother or foster mother, becomes the object of the child's deepest feelings, his psychological parent . . . The inescapable fact is that once a young child leaves the care of his family, however necessary that may be, he is emotionally at risk because of the rupture of his relationships. These will be broken again if, in due course, he has to give up a temporary caretaker to whom he has become attached, even to return to the mother. If leaving his family subjects him to a succession of caretakers, the risks to his emotional health are compounded.'*

Any form of temporary substitute care had come to be seen as detrimental to the development of especially young children. These ideas were contentious and were subjected to rigorous examination. While Clarke and Clarke,[7] Robertson and Robertson,[8] Bowlby[9] and Rutter[10] did stress the need for young children to remain in close contact with their parents for an effective bond to be maintained, nonetheless there was evidence that children were able to form and sustain attachment bonds with a number of different people.[11] Furthermore, Jenkins,[12] Holman,[13] Thorpe,[14] and Fanshel and Shinn[15] showed that lack of contact with birth parents was detrimental to the child's emotional growth and led to more disturbed behaviour. 'In the main,' Fanshel and Shinn concluded in 1978, 'we strongly support the notion that continued contact with parents, even when the functioning of the latter is marginal, is good for most foster children. Our data suggests that total abandonment by parents is associated with emotional turmoil in children.'[16]

Other studies stressed permanence as a developmental need and in consequence as a "right".[17] Rowe and Lambert made apparent the harmful effects when separation resulted in limbo and drift:[18]

> 'It is our conviction that no child can grow emotionally while in limbo, never really belonging to anyone except on a temporary and ill-defined or partial basis. He cannot invest except in a minimal way (just enough to survive) if tomorrow the relationship may be severed . . . To grow the child needs at least the promise of permanency in relationships and some continuity of environment.'

Later research produced equally worrying findings: children stayed in temporary foster care for long periods; children moved frequently between placements; the state of being a foster child was likely to destroy their relationships with their birth family; and children themselves found the temporary nature of their foster home a source of deep anxiety and concern.[19]

The 1970s–1980s: permanency planning – the least detrimental alternative

Although rehabilitation was still held to be the ideal, the possibility of it always being achieved was questioned. Rather than aim for the best outcome for children and fail, it might be better in some circumstances to seek instead the 'least detrimental alternative'. This was the view put forward by Goldstein, Freud and Solnit,[20] who believed that in child care practice 'the best was the enemy of the good'. They suggested that the laudable aim of rehabilitation was ignoring the prime need of children in care to live with parent figures with whom they could be sure they could remain. They urged social workers to seek instead the 'least detrimental alternative': stable parenting by "psychological parents" – either the foster carers with whom they were already living, or new parents willing to take on the role. They argued that for many children contact with birth parents tended to impede these attachments and render the placement vulnerable, and sanctioned a return to an "exclusive" model of substitute care.[21]

"Permanency planning" was a new approach to the provision of care for children, which had been developed in the USA (where over half of all foster children had typically been in temporary care for two years or more) in response to problems similar to those being experienced in the UK. This had shaped the philosophy, goals and services of child welfare agencies, re-forming them to accept the primacy of the needs of children over the "blood tie".[22]

The concept of permanency planning emerged in the publications of the Oregon Project on permanency planning. In November 1973, the Oregon Children's Services Division initiated a federally funded demonstration project designed to reduce the number of children placed inappropriately in foster care (in the USA this includes residential and family care). Known as the Oregon Project, it sought to reduce the backlog of children in indeterminate status by developing permanent alternatives. In a three year period, 509 children in 17 of Oregon's 36 counties were accepted by the project. The screening criteria required that the children were under 12 years of age, unlikely to return home, adoptable and that they had been in foster care for a year or more.[23]

The first step in attempting to find permanent homes was to explore the possibility of reuniting the children with their parents. Where return home was impossible, project caseworkers encouraged parents to relinquish their rights, or terminated parental rights, to free the children for adoption. When neither of these alternatives was possible a written contract with foster parents was formulated to provide the child with some degree of stability. At the end of the project, a quarter of the children had in fact returned to their parents. Another 36 per cent had been adopted, eight per cent were in contract foster care, and three per cent were with relatives. Only just over a quarter of them remained in foster care.[24]

The Oregon Project gave priority to children already placed in foster care. However, Maluccio and Fein[25] in 1983 saw permanency planning more broadly encompassing not only children and youth in foster care but also, and perhaps more importantly, those at risk of such placement. They defined permanency planning as the 'systematic process of carrying out, within a brief time-limited period, a set of goal-directed activities designed to help children live in families that offer continuity of relationships with nurturing parents or caretakers and the opportunity to establish lifetime relationships,' either in their own homes or placed permanently with other families. It was designed to deal with drift in out-of-home care, and emphasised decision making and assertive case management involving prompt, decisive, goal-directed action.[26]

The concept of permanency planning is built on a number of basic beliefs. It stresses the value of rearing children in a family setting, based on a belief in the primacy of the family in the child's growth and development, and in the continuing need of each human being to belong to a family and the significance of the family in "human connectedness". The primacy of the parent–child attachment is part of the rationale behind permanency planning,[27] which also emphasises the importance of stability in living arrangements, and of continuity, stability and mutuality in parent–child relationships.[28]

Permanency planning, therefore, stresses the need for continuity of parental relationships, but not necessarily with the biological parents. Indeed, Goldstein et al[29] advocated legislation to provide each child with a permanent relationship with those adults who functioned psychologically as his or her parents. This was not accepted without question; others have stressed the fundamental importance of the biological family in the child's life, i.e. the claim for the inherent advantages of the relationship between the biological parent and child.

Permanency planning also implies the right of every child to be provided with a stable home, quickly and with as few moves or temporary situations as possible. Adcock and White[30] expressed this belief very firmly: 'No child should be deprived of an opportunity to grow up either in his own family or in a new family which he can legally call his own, unless there is a very strong reason to justify this.'

Decision making is perhaps the most crucial component of permanency planning methodology. It consists of the process of actively and deliberately making choices between alternative options by following specific steps and procedures, so as to lead to a permanent plan for a child. The plan is decided upon and implemented within a reasonable length of time. It is recognised that time is of prime importance, and that decisions about where a child shall grow up need to be made quickly, taking, preferably, no longer than a year. It stresses the importance of adhering to time frames that assure children protection from a long time in drift or limbo.[31] Maluccio et al summed up the approach thus:

'In short, deliberate, purposeful, and aggressive decision making, even in the midst of uncertain or incomplete knowledge, is advocated in place of passive decision making through inertia or inaction which in the past has too often led to impermanence and the neglect of children in out-of-home care or at risk of such placement.'[32]

Although a major plank of permanency planning programmes was the comprehensive and intensive efforts to keep children in their own homes, nonetheless there was increased emphasis on plans for adoption, and consequently increasing dependency on the legal system.

Permanency planning – the response in the UK

The most novel aspect of these policies was the placement for adoption of children who had previously been considered unadoptable, principally older children and those with physical and mental disabilities, or emotional and behaviour difficulties.[33] The success of the Oregon Project led to further demonstration projects, and publicity spread to the UK, where it was the success in finding adoptive families which was most widely reported. Preventive work had already been judged to be less than successful, as had attempts at long-term foster care.[34]

The opening of the Barnardo's New Families Project in Glasgow in 1976 'heralded in a decade in which permanence policies would dominate the progressive thinking about meeting the needs of children in care'.[35] When permanency policies became part of child care practice in the UK it was, according to Thoburn, 'the adoption aspects of permanence which were to the fore, at the expense of preventive and rehabilitative aspects'.[36] Such policies, it was hoped, would minimise "drift" in unplanned care and cut down the numbers of young people leaving care at 18 who were attached to neither their birth families nor to substitute families. It aimed to give them, according to Triseliotis, 'a family for life, with its network of support systems not only for them but also for their future children'.[37]

The 1975 Children Act made adoption a more likely alternative for some children in long-term care, and both fostering and adoption were seen as options in a range of substitute family placements.[38] In the UK there had always been the possibility that children in long-term foster care could be adopted by their foster carers, but the 1975 Children Act strengthened the position of foster families considering adoption.[39] As adoption was to be considered an available option for a greater number of children in care, the adoption of children whose parents did not request it, and who might actively oppose it, became a possibility. Such an extension of the ranks of "adoptable" children was, and still is, highly controversial.

When permanency planning crossed the Atlantic it was translated into a model of child care social work which Thoburn described thus:[40]

> 'Social workers should make every effort to return children to their parents as quickly as possible, but parents who were reluctant to resume care of their children should not be pressed to do so, and the advantages of adoption for the child and for themselves should be pointed out to them. Plans for children in care should be explicit, and should be agreed by a more senior member of staff. A time limit appropriate to the age of the child should be agreed, after which a decision should be made to seek a permanent placement, preferably with an adoptive family.'

Morris identified a four-point philosophy guiding permanence policy in Britain:

i) children removed from their homes should be subject to temporary care for the shortest possible time;

ii) that the decision to return them home or to sever their ties with their parents should also be made within a short period of time (two year maximum);

iii) the single best alternative to returning the child home is to place the child with adoptive parents;

iv) foster care, where caretakers have neither custody nor guardianship, should be seen only as a temporary solution.[41]

A number of projects were established concerned with actively seeking permanent homes for children (notably Parents for Children, Barnardo's New Families Project Glasgow, New Black Families IAS/Lambeth Project, The Child Wants A Home, Adoption Resource Exchange, and BAAF's Be My Parent). Although "permanence" had figured highly in child care literature and thinking from the mid 1970s, it was not until the early 1980s that substantial numbers of children in care were placed with permanent substitute families in Britain.[42]

The unacceptable face of permanence

Since the mid 1970s permanence had been seen predominantly to refer to substitute family care. In the mid 1980s it was, however, acknowledged that the emphasis upon adoption had perhaps gone too far. The Report of the House of Commons Social Services Committee regretted this trend towards equating "permanence" with adoption:

> 'There is at the moment considerable confusion over the significance of the search for permanence in a placement. It should not have become a synonym for adoption. Adoption is only one eventual outcome among many. It is however, the most permanent possible outcome for a child unable to live with his natural family.'[43]

Permanence within the child's birth family did not seem to be as energetically pursued. The other significant conclusion of the *Children Who Wait*[44] study was that once a child was received into care the first six months were *crucial* both for planning and for work with the family as a whole, and within that period there was indeed a need for the development of 'radical and imaginative preventive and rehabilitative work'.[45]

Rowe, surveying foster care in the eighties,[46] suggested that one of the benefits of planning for permanence was the urgency and emphasis it brought to providing services to birth parents which would enable them to resume care of their children before they had put down roots elsewhere and developed bonds with psychological parents. Agencies which worked hard to achieve permanence reported a significant increase in rehabilitation of children to their birth families.

However, there were serious doubts as to whether enough was being done in this regard. Rowe also reported that conspicuous by its absence in most discussion of foster care was any adequate consideration of work with natural parents. American research by Jenkins and Norman,[47] and by Fanshel and Shinn,[48] revealed a lack of services to the child's family. Similar findings emerged in this country in reports by Aldgate, Rowe et al, and unpublished work by Thorpe.[49]

The belief that the same positive coverage was not given to the need for preventive and rehabilitative services in the UK was echoed by Packman in 1981.[50] It was feared this could mean a further decrease in the possibility for some children of being raised by their families of origin. Emphasis needed to be placed on preventing children becoming *isolated* from their families of origin as well as securing their future. Morris feared that in the rush for security the child's need for continuity with his or her family might be lost and his/her identity shattered.[51] Jordan expressed the same fear: 'The danger is that, in the climate of a shrinking role for the state, this model should be adopted without a commitment to prevention.'[52]

In 1986, Thoburn et al[53] voiced the concern that the move towards greater compulsion in child care in order to facilitate planning for permanence may have had the unforeseen consequence of a less appropriate and sensitive service to those who should go home. They suggested that an "ambulance service" for the rescue of a small number of casualties was preferred because it was cheaper than a preventive service for the far greater numbers at risk. Holman,[54] Stevenson,[55] and Jordan[56] urged that the gains for the small numbers of children in care who were placed for adoption should not be at the expense of those who would be vulnerable if more resources were not made available to them and their families.

In 1986 Millham et al[57] demonstrated that the majority of children coming into care did in fact eventually return to their birth families or move into independent living situations. Of the 170 children under six years on admission to care in this Dartington study, only 24 were in long-term care two years later. This finding was an important reminder that agencies, in initiating policies for the small numbers who needed permanent family placement, must take care that these did not result in inappropriate and unhelpful services to the far greater numbers who would eventually return to their parents and needed to be helped to do so as quickly as possible. Millham and his colleagues confirmed in a later study that 90 per cent of children and adolescents who are taken away from their families into the care of a local authority eventually go home.[58]

Consequently although the permanency movement had made great progress in terms of the successful placement of some children in permanent substitute care, it may also have had the effect of directing resources and attention away from other alternatives in child care social work, one of which was the imaginative and supportive use of short-term foster care. The majority of children entering care (around 60 per cent) were found – in the 1940s and 1950s by The Curtis Committee,[59] Bowlby,[60] and Gray and Parr,[61] and more recently by Millham et al,[62] and Rowe et al[63] – to require a very temporary stay in care on account of those foreseeable or unforeseeable events (illness, confinements, temporary family difficulties) which prevent families temporarily caring for their children. Rather than being seen as a positive resource providing care for these children, short-term foster care instead acquired an image of being a rather harmful but perhaps necessary period of limbo that enabled the process of assessment and review to take place in order that the right decision could be taken in terms of permanent placement.

The 1980s–1990s: the changing role of short-term foster care

The definitions provided by the British Association of Social Work (BASW) in 1982 in *Guidelines for Practice in Family Placement*,[64] identified short-term fostering as part of a range of family placements on a continuum from relief care for parents of "handicapped" children to adoption. The legal maximum of eight weeks for short-term foster placements was considered to extend to up to six or eight months in practice.

Earlier Shaw and Lebens[65] (see Chapter 2), suggested that a process of polarisation was occurring at either end of this care continuum. Definitions put forward by the British Agencies for Adoption and Fostering

(BAAF), also in 1982, reflect more this polarisation. BAAF suggested that there were then only two types of placements: "short-term", the definition of which depended on intent (ie. impermanent) rather than duration, though they would normally be expected to end within six months; and "long-term", in which all expected the arrangement to be permanent. The provision of straightforward temporary care to help families appeared to have been swallowed up in a system of permanency planning, which required short-term placements to assess need, prepare for rehabilitation (including "training" of natural parents), prepare for permanent substitute care, provide a bridge in between "permanent" placements, or between residential care and independent living, or to provide treatment.[66]

By the end of the 1970s, the role and purpose of short-term fostering appeared to have changed and expanded considerably. However, its significance in 'the temporary fostering of children who are in care for a matter of weeks or months in time of family crisis – an intelligent and humane use of community resources'[67] does indeed seem to have been under-estimated at this time. It is noteworthy that in her article, "Fostering In the 1970s and Beyond", Jane Rowe recognised that 'Most short-term and medium-term placements . . . can be used successfully for the relief of families under stress and for the treatment of many child or family problems. There are great and as yet untapped potentialities in this kind of fostering as part of community services.'[68]

Yet the examination of these potentialities in the subsequent booklet, *Fostering in the Eighties*,[69] is limited to a small number of specialist schemes catering largely for children with "special needs" or teenagers. A positive outcome of this period was the development of short-term task centred care. An example of this would be the Barnardo's Bridge Families Scheme, a model of specialist fostering providing preparation for a new permanent placement and assessment after a placement disruption.[70] Cooper's analysis in 1978[71] suggested that it was only in the areas of unplanned emergency placements (24 hour), and of respite care (largely been used to provide support to the parents of children with severe disabilities), where much had been done to develop short-term care as a positive service for children and their families.

However, it was in the early part of the 1980s that it began to be recognised that the philosophy of a clear-cut distinction between, on the one hand, family responsibility for the care of children and, if that were not possible, state responsibility and permanent substitute care on the other, was not necessarily providing children and families with the help they needed. It was disparagingly described as the "shape up or shove off" philosophy by Shaw and Hipgrave in 1983.[72] Pressure from groups representing the families of children in care mounted, along with a feeling that crucial decisions about children's futures should be in the hands of the legal system rather than individual social workers.

It was also recognised that all families, natural and substitute, could benefit from support and help on an ongoing basis. In 1980, Parker wrote 'Although the principle of shared care now seems to be widely accepted, progress in practical terms is still slow. There is a long tradition in this country that either the state assumes responsibility . . . or that families (usually the mother) are left to manage as best they can . . . We think that a rigid division between parental care and substitute care prevents the discovery of imaginative and effective ways of providing optimal care for children.'[73]

For children with disabilities, the use of short-term periods of relief care away from home had been accepted as a positive way to relieve stress and enhance families' coping skills. Webb[74] defined this concept of respite as an arrangement whereby parents can place their children for short periods while retaining the prime responsibility for them. The idea of extending a similar policy to other children at risk of coming into care was to find, in the Children Act 1989, a way into the legislation.[75]

At the level of policy the Short report,[76] which arose out of an inquiry by the Social Services Committee in 1984, put prevention in child care at the top of the agenda and introduced the idea of "respite" into general child care. This idea of using short-term care as a preventive measure to avoid permanent breakdown was in 1985 given further support in the results of a number of significant research studies commissioned by the government which were collated in *Social Work Decisions in Child Care*:[77]

'. . . *the researchers also refer to the potentialities of using short-term care as a means of preventing the permanent break-up of families by offering temporary relief. By implication, they point out that if care is to be used positively and beneficially it has to be one of a range of options and used as part of a plan. Admission should have a purpose and not be just a last resort.'*

The studies questioned the way that care had been viewed in an undifferentiated way as unhelpful. We have already seen in Chapter 1 that Packman et al[78] reported in 1986 that viewing admission to care as a "last resort" was sometimes found to be contributing to ill-planned, traumatic admissions and unstable placements, and also ignored the fact that some admissions were indeed experienced as helpful. Both Packman et al and Vernon and Fruin[79] found it necessary to differentiate on the basis of the reason for admission, separating "family service" from interventions based on the need to "rescue" the child or to protect others from the child's behaviour.

Following this, the idea of partnership between parents and social workers in the form of shared care was expressed in the 1987 White Paper which preceded the 1989 Children Act. It stated that local authority social services would be given 'a broad umbrella power to provide services to promote care . . . and to help prevent the breakdown of family relations . . . allowing for a child to stay for short or long periods away from home, say with a foster family or children's home.'[80] It was hoped to counteract the negative image of care as an outcome to be avoided at almost all costs. The White Paper underlined the positive aim of providing care away from the family home as a means of providing support to the family and reducing the risk of long-term family breakdown.[81]

In the Children Act 1989 this became the use of care away from home as a means of providing support under Part III of the Act, and was translated into the power to provide accommodation under Section 20. It supported the use of short-term care as a pro-active rather than a reactive means of offering preventive social work, and entailed a shift away from making prescriptive and value-laden judgements towards a new context in which both parents and social services have a conception of working together in partnership to promote the welfare of children well into the future.[82]

The 1990s – shifting the balance towards family support services
Some of these aims and ideals reflected in the Children Act 1989 have been slow to be realised for a number of reasons. Renewed concerns

about the level and seriousness of child abuse came to the forefront of attention at the very end of the 1980s. The publication of the first *Working Together*[83] document by the government focused the attention of both local authorities and voluntary agencies on issues relating to the protection of children, by providing clear guidelines and expectations about the way in which professionals from all agencies should work together to ensure good practice. Increasing understanding and knowledge about child abuse, and creating effective ways to protect children became a top priority, and has remained so in the early years of the implementation of the Children Act 1989.

Concerns have been expressed recently that this has led to a slower implementation of Part III of the Act, which deals with local authority support services for children and families, than Parts IV and V, which provide the legal framework for local authorities to intervene where they believe a child is suffering, or is likely to suffer significant harm. The Audit Commission[84] has recently carried out a national study of children's services and one of their findings was:

'Because of the pressure of child protection work field social workers have little spare time for work with other "children in need" who require support other than child protection.'

The Audit Commission suggests that we should set a new course in Social Services:

'The Children Act sets the agenda: to protect children from significant harm and, in partnership with parents and other agencies, to safeguard and promote their health and development. The strategies that authorities develop should translate these broad objectives into a balanced range of activities.'[85]

Another area that has been slow to develop is legislation to bring adoption law policy and practice in line with the Children Act 1989. At the beginning of the decade the Department of Health produced discussion papers for the Inter-Departmental Review of Adoption Law.[86] As part of this review the possibility of introducing a more "inclusive" form of adoption, termed "open adoption" was debated. Although in 1993 the White Paper[87] on proposed adoption legislation drew back from the suggestion, the move away from "exclusiveness" continues in practice as contact is now viewed to be in the interests of most children. There is the possibility of attaching Section 8 Contact Orders under the Children Act 1989 to Adoption Orders, as well as the suggestion that a new set of Placement Orders be introduced to bridge the gap between adoption and fostering.

The value of the "inclusive" model for most forms of substitute care has once again been recognised, and short-term or temporary foster placements may be able to offer a range of placement provision along part of the continuum from respite care to adoption consistent with the needs of children. We may now be some way towards achieving the vision for the future that Morris[88] put forward in 1984 when she urged that social workers:

> '. . . re-examine and expand the range of alternatives available to individual families in need of substitute family care – as a continuum – from preventive services precluding entry to care, through rehabilitative programmes involving short-term care only, to foster care with maintenance of family contact, to both open and closed adoption.'

The time is now ripe to consider the part that short-term fostering services can play in promoting and safeguarding the welfare of children.

References

1 George V, *Foster Care: Theory and practice*, Routledge & Kegan Paul, 1970.

2 Rowe J, and Lambert L, *Children who Wait*, ABAFA, 1973.

3 Department of Health & Social Security, *Report of the Committee of Inquiry into the Care and Supervision provided in relation to Maria Colwell*, HMSO, 1974.

4 Morris C, *The Permanency Principle in Child Care Social Work*, Social Work Monograph 21, University of East Anglia, Norwich, 1984.

5 Goldstein J, Freud A, and Solnit A J, *Beyond the Best Interests of the Child*, The Free Press: MacMillan, 1973, USA.

6 Robertson J, and Robertson J, 'The Psychological Parent', *Adoption & Fostering*, 87:1, 1977.

7   Clarke A, and Clarke A, *Early Experience: Myth and Evidence*, Open Books, 1976.

8   See 6 above.

9   Bowlby J, *The Making and Breaking of Affectional Bonds*, Tavistock Publications, 1979.

10 Rutter M, *Maternal Deprivation Reassessed*, (1st and 2nd edns) Penguin Books, 1972, 1981.

11 See 10 above for a summary of the evidence.

12 Jenkins R, 'Long term fostering', *Case Conference*, 15:9, 1969.

13 Holman R, *Trading in Children*, Routledge & Kegan Paul, 1973.

14 Thorpe R, 'The social and psychological situation of the long-term foster child with regard to his natural parents', unpublished PhD thesis, University of Nottingham, 1974.

15 Fanshel D, and Shinn E B, *Children in Foster Care: A longitudinal investigation*, Columbia University Press, 1978, USA.

16 See 15 above.

17 Summarised in 4 above.

18 See 2 above; Rowe, quoted in 4 above.

19 For a useful summary see 4 above.

20 See 5 above.

21 Thoburn J, Murdoch A, and O'Brian A, *Permanence in Child Care*, Blackwell, 1986.

22 Maluccio A N, Fein E, and Olmstead K A, *Permanency Planning for Children: Concepts and Methods*, Tavistock, 1986.

23 Lahti J, and Dvorak J, 'Coming home from foster care', in Maluccio A and Sinanoglu P (eds), *The Challenge of Partnership: Working with Parents of Children in Foster Care*, Child Welfare League of America, 1981, USA.

24 See 23 above.

25 See 22 above.

26 See 22 above.

27 Hess P, 'Parent–child attachment concept: crucial for permanence planning', *Social Casework*, 63:1, 1982, USA.

28 See 22 above.

29 See 5 above.

30 Adcock M, and White R (eds), *Terminating Parental Contact*, ABAFA, 1980.

31 See 22 above.

32 See 22 above.

33 Thoburn J, *Success and Failure in Permanent Family Placement*, Avebury/ Gower, 1990.

34 See 21 above.

35 See 33 above.

36 See 33 above.

37 Triseliotis J, "Identity and security in adoption and long-term fostering", *Adoption & Fostering*, 7:1, 1983.

38 Rowe J, *Fostering in the Eighties*, BAAF, 1983.

39 See 21 above.

40 See 21 above.

41 See 4 above.

42 See 33 above.

43 House of Commons, *Children in Care* (Short Report), Social Services Select Committee Report, HMSO, 1984.

44 See 2 above.

45 Hussell C, and Monaghan B, 'Child care planning in Lambeth', *Adoption & Fostering*, 6:2, 1982.

46 See 38 above.

47 Jenkins S, and Norman E, *Filial Deprivation and Foster Care*, Columbia University Press, 1972, USA.

48 See 15 above.

49 Aldgate J, Rowe J, et al, and unpublished work by Thorpe cited in 38 above.

50 Packman J, *The Child's Generation*, (2nd edn), Blackwell/Robertson, 1981.

51 See 4 above.

52 Jordan W, 'Prevention', *Adoption & Fostering*, 105, no 3 of 1981.

53 See 21 above.

54 Holman R, *Inequality in Child Care*, Child Poverty Action Group, 1976.

55 Stevenson O, 'Family problems and pattern in the 1980s', *Adoption & Fostering*, 4:2, 1980.

56 See 52 above.

57 Millham S, Bullock R, Hosie K, and Haak M, *Lost in Care: The problems of maintaining links between children in care and their families*, Gower, 1986.

58 Millham S, Bullock R, and Little M, *Going Home*, Dartmouth, 1993.

59 Home Office, *Report of the Care of Children Committee*, (Curtis Report), Cm 6922, HMSO, 1946.

60 Bowlby J, *Child Care and the Growth of Love*, (1st & 2nd edns), Penguin Books, 1953, 1965.

61 Gray P G, and Parr E A, *Children in Care and the Recruitment of Foster Parents*, COI, The Social Survey, 1957.

62 See 57 above.

63 Rowe J, Hundleby M, and Garnett L, *Child Care Now*, BAAF, 1989.

64 BASW, *Guidelines for Practice in Family Placement*, BASW, 1982.

65 Shaw M, and Lebens K, 'Children between families', *Adoption & Fostering*, 84, no 2 of 1976.

66 See 38 above.

67 See 52 above.

68 Rowe J, 'Fostering in the 1970s and beyond', ABAFA. Reprinted in Triseliotis J (ed), *New Developments in Foster Care and Adoption*, Routledge & Kegan Paul, 1980.

69 See 38 above.

70 Westacott J, *Bridge to calmer waters – a study of a Bridge Families Scheme*, Barnardo's, 1988.

71 Cooper J D, *Patterns of Family Placement*, National Children's Bureau, 1978.

72 Shaw M, and Hipgrave T, *Specialist Fostering*, Batsford/BAAF, 1983.

73 Parker R A (ed), *Caring for Separated Children*, Macmillan, 1980.

74 Webb S, 'Preventing reception into care; a literature review of respite care', *Adoption & Fostering*, 14:2, 1990.

75 Aldgate J, Pratt R, and Duggan M, 'Using care away from home to prevent family breakdown', *Adoption & Fostering*, 13:2, 1989.

76 See 43 above.

77 Department of Health & Social Security, *Social Work Decisions in Child Care*, HMSO, 1985.

78 Packman J, Randall J, and Jacques N, *Who needs Care? Social work decisions about children*, Blackwell, 1986.

79 Vernon J, and Fruin D, *In Care: A study of social work decision making*, National Children's Bureau, 1986.

80 Department of Health & Social Security, *The Law on Child Care and Family Services*, Cm 62, HMSO, 1987, para 18.

81 See 80 above.

82 See 74 above.

83 Department of Health & Social Security, *Working Together*, 1988.

84 Audit Commission, *Seen but not Heard*, HMSO, 1994.

85 See 84 above.

86 Department of Health, *Review of Adoption Law: Report to ministers of an interdepartmental working group*, 1990.

87 Department of Health/Welsh Office/Home Office/Lord Chancellor's Department, *Adoption: The Future*, CM 2288, HMSO, 1993.

88 See 4 above.

4 Attachment and separation

Studies of the psychological effects of the processes of attachment and separation have considerably influenced the development of fostering services. Bowlby's[1] theories of maternal deprivation were a key factor in the demise of residential care for very young children, and the promotion of fostering as the preferred method of care for all children deprived of a normal home life with their natural parents. Later, the preoccupation with the importance of an undisturbed family life for the developing child, especially the very young child, resulted in the emphasis shifting to the prevention of children coming into care at all, and fostering was no longer given the priority it had previously been afforded. Even temporary placements were considered to disrupt important bonds and were thus regarded as damaging to a child's development.

Whenever a child is placed in foster care, processes of both separation and attachment are likely to be occurring, and in a short-term or temporary placement similar processes will be at work on the child's return to their family or move to another placement. When children are "looked after" away from home, separation affects parents as well as children. The term "filial deprivation" was introduced by Jenkins and Norman,[2] as a corollary to maternal deprivation, 'to characterise the feelings and reactions of parents whose children have been taken or received into care.' The feelings of the parents, and the resulting blow to self-esteem, could affect their interaction with a child in care as well as their ability to resume care when the child returns home.

Knowledge and understanding of how these processes work could enable us to reduce the trauma of foster care for both children and parents, especially at the beginning and end of placements, and contribute to successful placement provision. This chapter explores the current state of the knowledge base, and examines how it can usefully be applied to the fostering situation.

Attachment and bonding

Attachment has been defined as 'a bond of mutual affection which links two people and which is evidenced by attachment behaviours.'[4] Attachment theory consists of a series of ideas about the value and effect of particular early social relationships, but it is not a precise science, and cannot be used to make predictions, nor as an explanatory concept. However, Vera Fahlberg[5] has comprehensively reviewed the relevance of attachment theory to child care. She has examined the way that attachment usually develops between parent and child, and how attachment and attachment behaviours vary with the age of the child.

In a paper to the World Health Organisation in 1951, Bowlby[6] drew attention to the symptoms observed in institutionalised and hospitalised children. Many exhibited disturbed behaviour, were intellectually retarded, and were unable to form close relationships with others. He believed that a child deprived of the opportunity to form bonds of affection with a mother or permanent mother substitute during the early years of life would develop social, emotional and or intellectual problems in later life. "Maternal deprivation" was the term he used to characterise this syndrome. Bowlby observed that it could lead to "affectionless psychopathy" – an inability to feel affection for or care about the well-being of others. Maternal deprivation could also lead to depression, enuresis and dwarfism.

Many years later, Bowlby[7] noted the universal occurrence of attachment behaviour. He described a young child's tendency to seek closeness to certain people and to feel secure when they are present. He found that infants were initially universally sociable, but began to demonstrate preferences around seven to eight months when the first strong attachments appeared to form. He observed that attachment behaviour included moving towards, staying close, clinging, protest at separation from, and using the adult as a "secure base" from which to explore. Bowlby suggested that early bonding to the mother was the essential precursor of later social relationships and formed the basis of all interpersonal relationships in later years. He laid particular stress on the need for continuity and was explicit that this could not be provided by a roster of residential care staff. He emphasised that particular care needed to be taken to ensure that alternative arrangements for mothering had regularity and continuity. He argued for the bias for a child to attach him or herself to one figure (monotropy), but this has not been proven. Later researchers stressed the importance of attachments which form with other adults, particularly the father.

In 1981, Rutter[8] provided a major re-assessment of Bowlby's work and a summary of the main research. He reported that Schaffer and Emerson in 1964 observed attachment behaviour of 60 babies. Like Bowlby they found that the first strong attachment to a particular person occurred around the age of seven to eight months, but they also found that most children formed attachments with many people – fathers, siblings, grandparents, family, and friends – and that bonds were often multiple. By 18 months only 13 per cent of the babies in their study had just one attachment figure. The remainder had formed multiple attachments of varying intensity, although there was usually one particularly strong attachment. The breadth of the attachments was largely determined by the social setting. They observed that the main bond was not always with the mother. Indeed a small group of infants were identified whose strongest attachments were with their fathers. They showed that "mother" could be male or female and that the role could be shared by several people. They found that any person who provides a great deal of stimulation and interaction could become an attachment figure, even if they are not providing food.

Cross-cultural studies of attachment have provided support for the notion of multiple attachments. Rutter also reported Ainsworth's 1967 study of the Ganda tribe in Uganda. This study lent support to Bowlby's earlier description of the course of attachment behaviour. However, the babies in Uganda were cared for by several adults in addition to their mothers, and most formed attachments simultaneously with several people. In 1977 Fox studied Israeli *kibbutzim*, where children were cared for in peer groups by caretakers called metapelets, only seeing their natural parents for a couple of hours a day. Nonetheless the children appeared to form stronger attachments to their mothers than to the caretakers with whom they spent so much time. They also developed strong bonds with their infant peers. Rutter suggested that Bowlby had underestimated the importance of the role of the father. He cited Belsky who, in 1979, found that mothers and fathers play different but complementary roles in the lives of their children. Rutter concluded that if mothering is of a high quality and is provided by figures who remain the same during the child's early life, then multiple mothering (at least up to four or five mother figures) need have no adverse effects.

Rutter also examined a number of studies to identify what circumstances are required for the development of attachments, again noting particularly the studies of Schaffer and Emerson in 1964, Schaffer in 1971 and 1977, and Ainsworth in 1974. He found that attachment took time – the same person had to have contact over a prolonged period. The intensity of the parental interaction with the child probably was important. Play and attention led to a more strongly attached child. Neither feeding nor caretaking were essential features – children could be mainly attached to someone who was not their main caregiver.

Adults who adapted their behaviour to the specific requirements of the individual infant were more likely to become attachment figures. This demonstrated the importance of maternal responsiveness, that is, sensitivity to the infant's and child's needs and signals. Attachment was also more likely with a person who provided comfort in distress. It was parental apathy and lack of response which appeared more important as inhibitors of the child's attachment. Attachments could be stronger when the child had few caretakers.

"Sensitive responsiveness" seemed to be the one quality in any interaction most likely to foster secure personal bonding. Parenting was described as a process of reciprocal interaction. The quality of attachment formed depended on the mother's sensitivity to a child's emotional needs. But if the mother figure responded less readily then the child would be more likely to develop "anxious attachment". Attachment does not presuppose a developmentally healthy relationship.

Rutter also found there was a strong case for distinguishing between attachment behaviours and bonding. He described attachment behaviour as the general tendency to seek attachments to other people, involving the need for proximity. It could be measured in behavioural terms. Bonding, however, represented a selective attachment that persisted over time, even during a period of no contact with the person with whom the bonds existed. Thus clinging, institutionalised children might have temporary attachments to caretakers, but not bonds, while at the same time retaining strong bonds to their mothers in spite of repeated or prolonged separations.[9]

Rutter distinguished secure bonds from those that are insecure; the more secure they are the more positive will be the greeting and following behaviour, with less crying on separation. The strength of bonding may be best determined by the degree of reduction of distress in a frightened situation when the bonded person is present. Aldgate has highlighted how anxiety and fear are emotions that many children will experience when separated from adults to whom they are attached.[10]

There has been a great deal of debate concerning the issue of whether or not there are specific times in a child's development when certain attachments must have been formed to result in healthy functioning. It has been argued that the first years of life are crucial in the development of attachments. Bowlby[11] proposed that there was a "critical period" or optimal time when the primary attachment should occur. He suggested that the first bonds must develop during the first two years or so if normal social relationships were to be possible later. However, later research has produced little evidence to support Bowlby's earlier claims of an early critical period for the formation of attachments.

In 1976 Clarke and Clarke[12] suggested that the whole of development is important, with the infancy period no more so than middle or later childhood. Tizard and Hodges[13] studied a group of institutionalised children who were later adopted. Initially two years old, the children were reassessed at the ages of four and a half, eight and sixteen years. The study provided information about the long-term outcomes of spending early childhood in residential care, and the long-term outcome of adoption after infancy. Tizard and Hodges found that the children were able to form strong attachments to their adoptive parents, but still had some emotional problems and difficulties at school and in peer relationships both at age eight and at age sixteen. Although the severe consequences of "affectionless psychopathy" predicted by Bowlby were not apparent, nonetheless the consequences of spending the first few years in residential care were considerable.

Rutter's summary of the research[14] refuted the notion that personality is fixed and unalterable by the end of the pre-school years. However, he also noted that although attachments can still develop for the first time after infancy, full normal social development might be dependent on early bonding. Environmental improvement which occured in middle or later childhood or adolescence could also be beneficial to a child's social and emotional development.

Thus Rutter supported the view that distortion of early child care may have adverse effects on psychological development, but objected to the term "maternal deprivation" to cover what is probably a wide range of different problems. He contended that the use of the term "maternal deprivation" to explain the consequences of so many different defects in child care is misleading. He was concerned to look at specific aspects of inadequate child care and their separate effects, distinguished between short-term and long-term effects of "maternal deprivation", and analysed the qualities of mothering necessary for normal development.

Rutter argued that a child needs love, the development of enduring bonds, a stable but not necessarily unbroken relationship, and a stimulating interaction (in addition to care and protection, discipline and guidance, food, models of behaviour, play, parent-child communication, and language). He concluded that it did seem particularly difficult for an institution to provide parental care of the quality and quantity expected in the family setting.

Separation and studies of maternal deprivation

The emphasis that has been placed on the need for continuity in relationships has been most influential in shaping child care practice. In his monograph published in 1951, Bowlby[15] argued that the young pre-school child was unable to maintain a relationship with a person in their absence and for that reason even brief separations disrupt a relationship. Experience with normal children would suggest that this is not always so, and it seems probable that environmental conditions, as well as age, influence a child's ability to maintain a bond during a person's absence. Rutter[16] questioned whether an unbroken relationship was entirely necessary to avoid discontinuity. He examined evidence to consider whether separation did in fact equate with discontinuity, and whether separation led to harmful effects both short and long term.

Rutter demonstrated that a child's reaction to separation depends on a number of factors and is in fact very complex. He contended it is not a question of whether children should separate from their mothers, but how and when separation should occur; transient separations are common, and certain sorts of happy separation may actually protect young children from the adverse effects of later separation.

Bowlby believed that separation involves a grief reaction; the loss of the person is crucial, not just the loss of maternal care. The short-term effect of separation has been identified as a characteristic immediate response called the "syndrome of distress". It is likely to be due to the disruption of the attachment process (but not necessarily with the mother). It has been most frequently studied where a child has been admitted to hospital or a residential nursery. It constitutes protest (immediate reaction of excessive distress and crying), followed by despair (misery and apathy), and finally by detachment (where the child apparently adjusts to the situation, appears content and disinterested in parents). Children who have never developed attachments seem not to show this syndrome of distress.

Children aged between six months and four years are most vulnerable to distress on separation, but this will also be affected by their temperament. Rutter examined the enormous variation in the way individuals react and made the following observations. The previous mother–child relationship was important as well as the child's previous separation experiences. A child's response to separation may be influenced for better or worse by the nature, of previous separations. The duration of separation needed to be considered, and whether separation also involved the child being in a strange environment, for the distress could be due to the environment rather than the separation as such. On the whole it appeared that separations may be less stressful if the infant remained in a familiar environment. Familiar people, other than the mother, also reduced children's distress in strange situations, related to the strength of the bond formation. It was separation from the family (or all people to whom the child is attached) which was important and not just separation from the mother. Circumstances during the separation could also affect the child's reaction. Stress could be reduced by providing stability, affection, active involvement, toys, and environmental stimulation. Separation could involve more distress if accompanied by changes in the maternal behaviour and the mother–infant relationship.

The acute distress syndrome was seen to have two phases: the distress during the separation, and later the disturbance on returning home afterwards. It has long been observed that children may be difficult and hostile as well as clinging after returning home from hospital, and it appears that the parental response to this behaviour may be crucial.

Reducing the impact of separation

Physical, psychological and emotional stages of development are important factors to be considered in determining which actions will minimise the effects of separation. Fahlberg[17] showed that the effect of separation depended upon the age of the child and the developmental tasks that needed to be accomplished at that stage, and upon the child's verbal and intellectual skills. The child's experience of separation was inevitably linked to an ability to retain the memory of the absent parent or to recall the experience of previous separations and their outcome.

Fahlberg stressed the need to assess the strength and nature of children's attachments when helping children move from one caretaker to another. That some children escape damage and some do not has long been observed, but the differences in vulnerability, or resilience, have been regarded as largely inexplicable. Aldgate[18] considered the relevance and application of attachment theory for work with children who have experienced faulty or unresolved severed attachments, and the characteristics which affect their reactions to loss and separation.

Rutter[19] provided evidence that it may be the infant–mother relationship prior to separation which influenced the infant's response to separation. In addition, in 1951 Freud and Dann[20] noted in their case study the protective effect of sibling relationships, and in 1965 Heinecke and Westheimer[21] also found the presence of a child (even very young siblings) could serve to reduce anxiety in stress situations.

Separation and bond disruption need not be regarded as synonymous. Rutter argued that the emphasis on the supposedly deleterious effects of all separations may have been misleading. Separation may or may not be harmful according to its effects on bonds and on attachment behaviour. He noted that the child needed to have the presence of a person to whom he or she is attached, but it was irrelevant whether or not this person was the mother. The child also needed adequate maternal care – but this need not be given by the person to whom the child was most attached. If so it was in a child's interest to encourage attachment to several people so that if one person was absent, another could take their place, though there can be some stress at the disruption of one of many bonds.[22]

Rutter described how the Robertsons' films of children in brief separation showed that the effects of separation could be ameliorated by improving maternal care during the separation: children cared for in a family showed some response to their separation, but not the same acute distress reaction seen in children admitted to hospital. The Robertsons were familiar to the children and the situation allowed new attachments to develop through personal and continuing interaction.

Rutter concluded that separation protest tended to be greater in strange circumstances than in familiar situations, and tended to be reduced if the child had the opportunity to form new attachments. It could be possible, by having some of the family present and by trying to keep the child's familiar routines as much as possible, to help reduce the likelihood of emotional disturbance.

The factors involved with disturbance following reunion are probably somewhat different from those operating at separation. What evidence there is suggests that disturbance is a consequence of the fact that separation serves to disturb and increase tensions in the mother–infant relationship. It would seem, Rutter suggests, that an increase in "mothering" at this time may facilitate a return to normality. Jenkins[23] referred to Bowlby's earlier description of the "vicious circle" resulting from unsympathetic handling by the mother when the returned child displays regressive, anxious behaviour: "bad behaviour" brings rebuffs and these rebuffs result in further "bad behaviour".

Separation can act as a precipitant but it appears that it is the more enduring problems in relationships which cause children's disordered behaviour. Chronic family adversity seems to render children more likely to be damaged by hospital admission, and disturbance is more likely if the child comes from a deprived or disturbed family or if the previous parent–child relationship was poor.[24]

Long-term effects of transient separations have also been considered. Rutter evaluated several investigations of short-term separations (usually a month or more) in early childhood. The studies reported little in the way of cognitive, emotional or behavioural ill effects, except a slightly increased risk of later psychological disturbance.[25] Separations for other reasons such as a holiday or admission to hospital had no measurable ill effects.

Rutter concluded that single isolated stresses in early life only rarely led to long-term disorder; that multiple acute stresses more often did so; and that long-term damage was most likely against a background of chronic adversity. This underlines the importance of considering the circumstances of the separation when deciding whether it is likely to be harmful or beneficial. Breaks are frequently associated with other adverse factors and it remains to be established whether it is the separation as such which is the deleterious influence.[26]

Wolkind and Rutter[27] found that children admitted for short periods into the care of a local authority later showed much deviance and disorder, but this group of children had been at a social and biological disadvantage from birth and their transient separation from home was but a minor episode in a long history of disturbing life experiences. Foster care was just one factor in the life experiences of severely deprived children – separation was not necessarily the key ingredient in their deprivation.

Most of the long-term effects are likely to be due to the lack (privation) of something rather than the loss of something (deprivation). It is the failure to develop bonds with *anyone*, not just the mother, that is important, as the chief bond need not be with a biological parent and need not be with a female. Family discord and the lack of a stable relationship with a parent, and lack of stimulation and necessary life experiences are likely to lead to long-term disturbance or developmental delay. Trasler[28] found in 1960 that prolonged institutional care in early life was the factor most likely to lead to subsequent breakdown of fostering and was the condition most likely to lead to affectionless detachment.

The distinction between failure to form bonds and bond disruption is important in understanding long-term effects. The failure to form bonds has been linked with the development of affectionless psychopathology. Bond disruption, however, causes distress which can be reversible.[29] Separation from all familiar people, or care which does not allow attachments, are also likely to be stressful to a young child. Rutter pointed out that substitute care for children separated from their families frequently involved both.

Nevertheless, knowledge of the processes of attachment and separation and about children's development can be, and in the best practice, has been, applied to the fostering situation to ameliorate the trauma of separation. Solnit[30] set out a scenario of temporary fostering which would successfully incorporate protective factors to minimise distress and the likelihood of maternal deprivation.

'When it is well done, the child is placed with foster parents who understand the advantage of regular visits from the parents, the frequency being determined by the child's developmental tolerances and capacities. That is, frequency, duration, and content of the visits by the natural parent are designed to maintain their relationship as psychological parents, while the foster parents are temporary substitutes who allow the child or children to relate to them without fear of displacing the natural parents. When such foster placement takes place as it does all too infrequently, the children have additional parents rather than the loss and replacement of parents. The additional parents should try to provide a continuity of environments, including familiar objects and patterns of care borrowed from natural parents. This implies an alliance, ideally, between natural and foster parents. In this way foster care supports the child's relationship to his parents with toys, food, sleeping and toiletting arrangements that help to reinforce a psychological presence; it also gives continuity of parents and a family setting that are temporarily replaced and supplemented by foster parents and a foster family.'

Much has been learned about reducing the trauma of admission to care from direct experiences recounted by parents, caretakers and social workers. A study by Aldgate[31] in the early 1970s confirmed that children's reactions to reception into care were influenced by the stage of their development and their previous life experiences, and even the most secure children experienced some trauma. However, she argued that this trauma could be decreased by continuity and by preparation for care. She stressed the value of preplacement visits, and that careful preparation of parents and children for separation was often the first significant step in bringing about their eventual reunion.

Preparation of foster carers to understand the reactions of children and parents is also crucial. Aldgate described what can happen when this is not done. Sometimes, she found, caretakers seemed to have little understanding of children's normal reactions to separation and colluded with parents anguish by making comments like 'he only cries when you come to see him'. Faced with such an unwelcome burden of responsibility it was little wonder that parents agreed to stop visiting in order to allow the child to "settle". This philosophy affected all children negatively but was especially dangerous for the very young. Deprived of frequent contact the under fives became detached from their parents remarkably quickly.[32]

Aldgate's study also provided important insights into the process of rehabilitation and reattachment. The further separation a child experienced on returning to his or her parents confronted him or her with 'the reawakening of early separation anxieties superimposed on current stress'. She found that although children's first reactions on hearing that they were to return were generally ones of delight, this could be followed by strong feelings of anger towards parents who had placed them in care, and depression from guilt about the anger. Children might also regret leaving the substitute family to whom they had become attached. Jenkins[33] also found evidence that the family may handle the separation by closing ranks behind the placed child, so that there was neither psychological nor physical space for the return.

Research evidence has stressed the importance of parents visiting children in foster care. Fanshel and Shinn[34] in their study found parents' visits to children in care to be the single variable predictive of return home. The importance of contact (or as it was then, access) as a necessary (but not sufficient) condition for the child's eventual return was also demonstrated by Aldgate,[35] and again by the research team at Dartington in the early 1980s.[36] The substantial research on foster care that supports parental visiting leads to a more open system of care, in which foster carers and biological parents are not sealed off from each other but can be helped to communicate around the needs of the children.[37]

Acceptance of multiple caretakers may also lead to a reconsideration of the role of foster carers in relation to birth parents; new approaches to shared care may indeed be perfectly viable. If it is accepted that the bond with the birth parent could be retained at the same time that appropriate attachments are made to a substitute carer, a whole series of options opens up for different models of foster care.

In the field of divorce there is new attention to joint custody as a viable solution. Studies by Wallerstein and Kelly[38] supported the view that children of divorced parents did best when there was access to both parents. The birth parent of the child in care could be seen as the equivalent of the non-custodial parent. Indeed, it was the recognition in the 1980s of the viability of a variety of lifestyles and forms of family life,[39] including models from a variety of ethnic groups, that contributed to the inclusion in the Children Act 1989 of measures that allow a number of different adults to play a significant part in a child's upbringing and development, particularly the concept, in both private and public law, that "parental responsibility" can be shared.

Filial deprivation

The work of Jenkins and Norman[40] highlighted in 1972 the fact that parents also experience feelings of anxiety and depression, followed by detachment, on separation from their children. Jane Aldgate[41] found that parents reacted to being prematurely separated from their children; reactions varied but all were concerned about their children's welfare. More recently, a number of research studies commissioned in the 1980s[42] included interviews with parents regarding the experience of their children's reception into care, and have been invaluable in affording practitioners an understanding of the parental perspective in the care process.

The separation experiences of parents when children enter care have been termed "filial deprivation". How parents were able to express these feelings was found to be indicative of the likelihood of rehabilitation; Jenkins and Norman[43] found that parents who were able to externalise emotions at reception into care were more able to effect rehabilitation than those who internalised emotions. Their research clearly pointed to the ambivalence of parents' feelings at the time of reception into care: the capacity to feel both sad and happy at the same time. Parents' sadness, emptiness and loneliness at separation was sometimes masked by thankfulness and relief, a thoroughly understandable emotion given that for many parents further stress could not have been tolerated. The situations of the families prior to placement showed that for the most part they were functioning at a marginal level. This was especially true of single parent households who formed a high proportion of families in the study.

Multiple problems existed in most of the families before placement. The large majority of reasons for the child entering care were family based rather than child based, especially in the case of younger children. Indeed many of the expressed parental feelings related very much to people and factors other than the child. It was self, other adults, agencies, and society in general to which most parents' strong feelings were directed. It was possible in the morass of interpersonal and social problems faced by these parents to overlook their specific feelings about the child and about the parent–child relationship.

Nonetheless, sadness was the feeling most frequently reported, along with worry and nervousness. Other feelings identified by parents were emptiness, anger and bitterness, guilt and shame; a small number were numb or paralysed. Little difference in feeling was expressed by mothers and fathers, and the feelings were relevant to the reason for placement and to how necessary the mother felt the placement to be. Three main clusters were identified: mothers who were primarily relieved and thankful; mothers who were mainly worried; and mothers who were mainly angry and bitter.

That parents are likely to feel overwhelmed and helpless in the face of a mass of feelings and problems has implications for social work in maintaining the parent–child bond. Aldgate[44] found that for many parents the prospect of reunion with their child might awaken old feelings of guilt and inadequacy. They feared their children might be like strangers, and found it hurtful that their children might wish to retain links with their substitute families.

Thoburn[45] suggested that parents may need help in attributing due importance to themselves and to their relationship with the child:

> *'Thus both while they are separated and especially when they come together after separation, parents and children are likely to need reinforcement about their worth, which can best come from satisfying relationships with those they care about.'*

Thoburn stressed the value of support to the family at this time and cited a number of ways in which it could be provided. This may be particularly necessary because, as Jenkins[46] pointed out, parents who fail tend to become objects of scorn in the community, and placement has often been seen as the admission of such failure.

Understanding and recognising the dynamics of the separation experience helped define the need for social work with the parents of children in care. The HMSO Guide in 1976 to practice in foster care[47] pointed out that parents' anxiety and concern to act positively on the child's behalf would be most intense when separation was either imminent or had just occurred. Within a very short time anxiety would give way to depression, soon to be counteracted and rationalised by detachment. Once detachment established itself, the parents might begin to reorganise their lives so that they actively excluded the child. The Guide stressed the importance of working intensively with parents about to be, or who had been very recently separated from their children.

References

1   Bowlby J, *Maternal Care and Mental Health*, World Health Organisation, 1951.

2   Jenkins S, and Norman E, *Filial Deprivation and Foster Care*, Columbia University Press, 1972, USA.

3   Thoburn J, *Child Placement: Principles and Practice*, Wildwood House/Gower, 1988.

4 Shaw M, and Hipgrave T, *Specialist Fostering*, Batsford/BAAF, 1983.

5 Fahlberg V, *A Child's Journey through Placement*, BAAF, 1994.

6 See 1 above.

7 Bowlby J, *Attachment and Loss: Volume 1, Attachment*, Penguin Books, 1969.

8 Rutter M, *Maternal Deprivation Reassessed*, (1st and 2nd edns) Penguin Books, 1972, 1981.

9 Jenkins S, 'The tie that bonds', in Maluccio A, and Sinanoglu P (eds), *The Challenge of Partnership: Working with parents of children in foster care*, Child Welfare League of America, 1981, USA.

10 Aldgate J, 'Work with children experiencing separation and loss: A theoretical framework', in Aldgate J, and Simmonds J, *Direct Work with Children*, BAAF/Batsford, 1988.

11 See 1 above.

12 Clarke A, and Clarke A, *Early Experience: Myth and Evidence*, Open Books, 1976.

13 Tizard B, and Hodges J, 'Research: Ex-institutional children: a follow-up study to age 16', *Adoption & Fostering*, 14:1, 1990.

14 See 8 above.

15 See 1 above.

16 See 8 above.

17 See 5 above.

18 Aldgate J, 'Attachment theory and its application to child care social work – an introduction', in Lishman J (ed), *Handbook of Theory for Practice Teachers in Social Work*, Jessica Kinglsey, 1991.

19 See 8 above.

20 Freud A, and Dann S, 'An experiment in group upbringing', *Psychoanal. Stud. Child.*, vol 6, 1951.

21 Heinecke C, and Westheimer I, *Brief Separations*, Longmans, 1965.

22 See 8 above.

23 See 9 above.

24 See 8 above.

25 See 8 above.

26 See 8 above.

27 Wolkind S, and Rutter M, 'Children who have been "in care" – an epidemiological study', *Journal of Child Psychiatry and Psychology*, 14, 1973.

28 Trasler G, *In Place of Parents: A study of foster care*, Routledge & Kegan Paul, 1960.

29 See 9 above.

30 Solnit A J, 'Least harmful to children', *Adoption & Fostering*, 87, 1977.

31 Aldgate J, 'Identification of factors influencing children's length of stay in care' in J Triseliotis (ed), *New Developments in Foster Care and Adoption*, Routledge & Kegan Paul, 1980.

32 See 31 above.

33 See 9 above.

34 Fanshel D, and Shinn E B, *Children in Foster Care: A longitudinal investigation*, Columbia University Press, 1978, USA.

35 See 31 above.

36 Millham S, Bullock R, Hosie K, and Haak M, *Lost in care: the problems of maintaining links between children in care and their families*, Gower, 1986.

37 See 9 above.

38 Wallerstein J, and Kelly J, *Surviving the Breakup*, Basic Books, 1980.

39 Rapoport R, Fogarty M, and Rapoport R N, (eds), *Families in Britain*, Routledge & Kegan Paul, 1982.

40 See 2 above.

41 See 31 above.

42 Department of Health & Social Security, *Social Work Decisions in Child Care*, HMSO, 1985.

43 See 2 above.

44 See 31 above.

45 See 3 above.

46 See 9 above.

47 Department of Health & Social Security, *Foster Care – A guide to practice*, HMSO, 1976.

5 The empirical study – overall patterns

The aims of the study

This empirical study aimed to demonstrate how short-term foster homes were being used, and to provide information about the nature of the placements, the characteristics of the children and their families, and the social work intervention. It also sought to identify factors that were significantly different between the children who went home quickly (within three months), and those who required a much longer stay in temporary care (up to two years and more); and to highlight those factors which might be used at the time of placement to distinguish children requiring a short placement from those who need a longer stay.

The information on which the study is based was obtained prior to the implementation of the Children Act 1989. Therefore, in reporting the study, terminology relevant to the old legislation is used to describe the legal status of the children. Thus all the children were "in care": children in "voluntary care" were placed under Section 2 of the Child Care Act 1980; others were "in care" compulsorily under a range of legal orders. Consequently the study talks of "admission" to care and "discharge" from care.

Following the implementation of the Children Act 1989 all children in local authority foster care are "looked after", but only those under legal orders are "in care". Children placed with foster carers on a voluntary basis are now "accommodated" under Section 20 of the Children Act. A proportion of the children in this study were Wards of Court. Such children would now be placed under the range of orders available under the Children Act 1989, as it is no longer possible for local authorities to use wardship. They would correspond to children whose cases are now being heard in the High Court rather than at Magistrates or County Court level.

The value of the study lies in recording in detail how an existing service was being used under the previous legislation, enabling an evaluation to be made of its relevance and usefulness following the implementation of the Children Act 1989.

Methodology

The study looked at 183 short-term foster placements made by Newcastle upon Tyne Social Services Department (SSD). This sample was obtained by taking every placement of a child made with approved short-term foster carers in a twelve month period between 1 August 1988 and 31 July 1989. The focus of the study was the use of short-term foster care, so that every placement could be included and analysed in the same way. If a child had two or more placements in the study period, information was obtained and analysed about each. If two or more siblings were placed together, each child was counted as one placement, and information was obtained and analysed about each. There are, therefore, more placements than children.

The SSD's records provided data on the age and gender of the children, their legal status, the length of placement, the placement outcome and the Area Team responsible for the placement; these are analysed in this chapter. At that time, information about ethnicity was not routinely recorded and monitored, but was included in the more detailed information obtained, by means of a questionnaire, on a sub-sample of the placements, consisting of 104 placements made between February and July 1989. Those results are reported in the following chapter.

Age of child at placement

The study found that short-term foster care was being used predominantly for very young children. Just over three-fifths of the placements were of pre-school children, that is, those aged four years and under, and 17 per cent of the placements were of children under one year old. Less than one-tenth of the placements were of children over the age of 12 years.

The age profile of children in short-term foster care differed from that of children in care overall, the latter being heavily weighted towards older children. Half of all children in the care of Newcastle upon Tyne SSD on 31 March 1988 were over 14 years old. Only a third of the children in short-term foster homes were aged ten years and over, compared to two thirds of the children in long-term foster homes.[1]

Table 1

Age of children at placement

Age in years	Frequency	Per cent	Cumulative %
0–4	115	63%	63%
5–9	36	20%	83%
10–14	21	11%	94%
15–17	11	7%	100%
	(n=183)		

Note: Percentages may not total 100 due to rounding

As end-of-year figures have not adequately reflected the considerable use of short-term foster homes for very young children, it is more useful to look at figures demonstrating the turnover of children in care when surveying short-term fostering. Although on 31 March 1988 there were only 68 children in short-term foster care compared to 210 in long-term foster care,[2] this study showed that over a twelve month period there were almost as many short-term foster placements (183) as children in long-term foster homes.

Short-term admissions of young children formed an important and growing proportion of the child care workload of social services departments, especially when the amount of work involved in effecting admissions and discharges is taken into account. The majority (58 per cent) of admissions to care in the 12 months ended on 31 March 1988 in Newcastle upon Tyne were of children under ten.[3] The rate of admissions to care was fairly stable while the total number of children in care in England continued to fall. Rowe et al[4] pointed out in 1989: 'There is evidently a more rapid turnover of care cases now and workloads will not have decreased in the way the statistics about children in care might lead people to expect.' As we saw in the Introduction, the trend towards a greater number of short placements appears to be continuing today.

Age and gender
Overall, there were more placements of girls than of boys – 54 per cent

of the placements were of girls, and 46 per cent were of boys. There were almost equal numbers of placements of boys (77) and girls (74) aged 0–9 years, but above that age, the short-term placements were overwhelmingly of girls. Short-term foster care was hardly being used at all for teenage boys in spite of the predominance of adolescent boys over adolescent girls in care. Nearly 75 per cent of the placements of children aged 10–14 years and 91 per cent of the placements of young people aged 15–17 years were of girls. Of the total sample of 183 placements, only seven were of boys aged ten and over, and only one of these was a boy aged 15–17 years.

Short-term foster care was not much used for teenage admissions. In Newcastle upon Tyne in the year ending 31 March 1988, 57 boys and 50 girls aged ten and over (excluding remands) were admitted to care,[5] but this study showed only seven short-term foster placements of boys aged 10–17, and 32 of girls aged 10–17, and at least nine of these were not new admissions but moves within the system of girls already in care at the time of placement. This pattern of minimal use of foster care for teenagers was also noted in the *Child Care Now* study in 1989: 'In spite of the current emphasis on family care most adolescents still go into residential establishments of some sort.'[6]

Length of placement

The overwhelming majority of placements were indeed very short, but a significant number lasted considerably longer (see Table 2). Seventeen per cent had ended within a week, and by far the largest number of placements (47 per cent) lasted for only one month or less; three-fifths had ended in two months; 70 per cent of the placements lasted three months or less. Only a small proportion of placements lasted longer than this but they lasted anything from four months to the longest placements of 17 months which were still ongoing at the time of analysis.* This pattern is consistent with the "leaving care curve" (see Chapter 1), with

---

*In all, 85 per cent of placements had ended by the time the data was analysed. This was just 18 months after the commencement of the study. Twenty seven placements were still ongoing, and have been included in the analysis on the basis of their length at that time. They were considerably longer on completion.

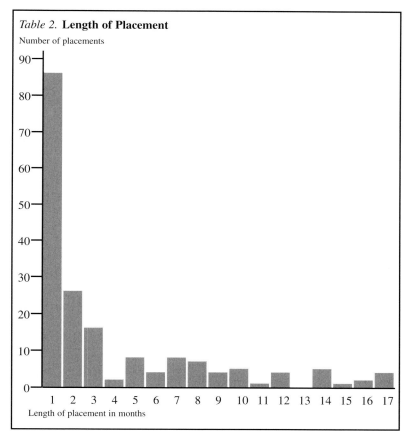

Table 2. **Length of Placement**

Number of placements

Length of placement in months

Note: For placements of 6 months or less, length is at completion of placement; 27 of the 41 longer placements were ongoing at time of analysis, and are included to show their length at that time

a high rate of discharges in the first few weeks, diminishing rapidly to a trickle, with a minority remaining in care indefinitely.

At the time of analysis, 12 (6.5 per cent) placements in this study had already lasted over a year, of which 11 were still ongoing. About a sixth of the placements (29) had lasted between seven and 12 months and of these 16 were still ongoing. In other words many of the already long "short-term" placements were destined to get even longer. In contrast only 7.5 per cent of placements (14) lasted between four and six months. It is evident that it is equally true for short-term foster placements that if the placement has not ended within a few weeks it has a very high chance of continuing for some considerable time.

Length of placement and the age of the child
There are interesting differences between the age groups and age is an important factor in the likely length of a child's placement. Table 3 shows that very high proportions both of children aged 0–9 and also of older adolescents experienced a short placement lasting three months or less. Notably, though, less than half of the placements of younger teenagers aged 10–14 ended within three months.

Very few children aged five and over experienced a placement lasting between four and six months. Twelve out of the fourteen placements which lasted between four and six months were of children aged 0–4 years. These observations would suggest that, if their placement has not ended within three months, children of five and over may be particularly likely to linger long in short-term placements, especially those aged 10–14.

Because short-term fostering is largely a service for very young children, however, the bulk of placements lasting over six months, in terms of numbers, were of 0–four-year-olds (25 placements). A temporary placement of over six months is a very significant part of a pre-school

Table 3

Age of child at placement and length of placement

| | Age in years | | | |
	0–4	*5–9*	*10–14*	*15–17*
3 months or less	69%	83%	48%	82%
4–6 months	10%	–	10%	–
7–12 months	13%	14%	33%	18%
Over one year	8%	3%	10%	–
	(n=115)	(n=36)	(n=21)	(n=11)

Note: Percentages may not total 100 due to rounding

child's life and likely to present a serious disruption in continuity. The special circumstances of these vulnerable young children need particular attention.

Length of placement and the gender of the child
There was a detectable, but not statistically significant, difference in the patterns of length of placements of boys and of girls as more of the shorter placements were of girls, and more of the longer placements were of boys. To some extent this bias may be caused by the preponderance of girls in the older adolescent age range whose placements ended largely within three months.

Legal status
Short-term foster care was predominantly used for children in voluntary care. In approximately four-fifths of the placements the children were in voluntary care, and in one-fifth they were in some form of compulsory care, either under a legal order or under wardship. Children who were subject to a Place of Safety Order, a Care Order (or Interim Care Order), or a Section 3 Resolution (Child Care Act 1980), have been grouped together as children "in care under orders", that is, in care under some

Table 4

Legal status at placement

	Frequency		Per Cent	
	Whole sample	*Sub-sample*	*Whole sample*	*Sub-sample*
Voluntary care – Total (Section 2)	**143**	80	**78%**	77%
In care under orders – Total	**23**	11	**13%**	11%
Place of safety	**7**	6	**4%**	6%
Care order (or interim)	**15**	4	**8%**	4%
Section 3 resolution	**1**	1	**1%**	1%
Wardship – Total	**17**	13	**9%**	12%
	(n=183)	(n=104)		

form of compulsion. Children under wardship have been analysed separately. Table 4 shows the details of the legal status of the children at placement, which would suggest that short-term foster care is a potentially important resource for children in need now requiring accommodation under Section 20 of the Children Act 1989.

The pattern is not untypical of overall child care admissions in Newcastle upon Tyne. According to statistics provided by the Department of Health, in the twelve months ending on 31 March 1988, 78 per cent of children admitted to care were in voluntary care, 13 per cent were Wards of Court, and only nine per cent were under a Care Order or Interim Care Order.[7] Given that a number of research studies commissioned in the early 1980s showed that compulsory powers (in particular Place of Safety Orders) were being used increasingly but were often counter-productive,[8] these findings were encouraging and consistent with the national picture. Rowe et al[9] reported in 1989 that two-thirds of admissions in their study were voluntary overall, rising to almost three-quarters of children aged under 11. However, as children remained in care they were increasingly likely to become subject to compulsory powers.[10]

Legal status at placement and length of placement
That there is a link between legal status and length of stay in care has already been established.[11] This study confirmed that legal status was also a significant factor in the length of short-term foster placements. Nearly four-fifths of the placements of children in voluntary care had ended within three months compared to less than a third of the placements of children in care under orders. Children in voluntary care accounted for 87 per cent of placements lasting three months or less. Less than one-fifth of the children in voluntary care stayed over six months in the placement, compared with half of the children in care under orders. Nonetheless, a number of placements of children in voluntary care did last longer, and accounted for almost two-thirds of the placements lasting over six months.

So although legal status is clearly important, on its own it is not very useful as a factor in predicting placement length. Roughly one-sixth of the children – both on a voluntary basis and under care orders –

experienced very lengthy temporary placements in "short-term" foster care. One-fifth of the placements of children in voluntary care lasted much longer than three months and some for well over a year. Even though the majority of children in care under orders experienced a longer temporary placement, some needed very short placements, perhaps a respite care break for long-term foster carers, or for birth parents where a child in care was placed at home, or whilst the child awaited a residential or assessment resource.

Legal status and the age of the child
The study showed that children at either end of the age scale were more likely to be in care under orders. Only six out of ten teenagers aged 15–17 were in voluntary care compared to nine out of ten children aged 5–9. Wardship was largely used for 0–4-year-olds.

Legal status and the gender of the child
There were no significant differences in the legal status of boys and girls in the sample. The percentage of children in voluntary care was almost exactly the same for both genders. A very slightly smaller percentage of boys were wards of court, and there were proportionately slightly more boys in compulsory care.

Placement outcome
Placement outcome has been a major focus of most studies of fostering

Table 5

Age of child and legal status at placement

| | Age in years | | | |
	0–4	5–9	10–14	15–17
Voluntary care	76%	89%	81%	64%
In care under orders	14%	8%	10%	18%
Wardship	10%	3%	10%	18%
	(n=115)	(n=36)	(n=21)	(n=11)

since Trasler's study[12] of long-term fostering in 1960. Many studies[13,14,15,16] have evaluated success and failure in fostering on the basis of placement breakdown because of concern about the harmful effects on children of what is now more usually called "disruption". Prior to this study, two studies – those by Berridge and Cleaver in 1987[17] and Rowe et al in 1989[18] – had included an examination of short-term or temporary placements. Rowe et al evaluated outcome in terms of how well placements met their aims, lasted as required, or were "helpful" to the child.[19] These categories are rather more suitable to the study of short-term fostering since it is hard to assess breakdown in placements that were anyway intended to end.

In the present study placement outcome is being used as a descriptive term and is intended to show how short-term fostering fitted into the wider processes of public child care provision. Most of the placements (85 per cent) had actually ended at the time of analysis, and it was possible to obtain information about where each child moved to.

The majority of placements (58 per cent) ended in the child's return home (or a move to independent living). Only 14 per cent resulted in a move to a permanent substitute family either for adoption or long-term fostering, 12 per cent of placements ended in a move to another temporary care placement, either a residential placement or another short-term foster home, and 15 per cent were still ongoing at the time of analysis.

Placement outcome and the age of the child
Whether or not a child returned home at the end of placement did appear to be clearly related to age. Only one placement of a child aged 15–17 years resulted in a return home, and only a third of those aged 10–14 returned home. This compares with 59 per cent of 0–4-year-olds and 83 per cent of children aged 5–9 years who were reunited with their families. These results are shown in Table 6.

The number of teenagers being admitted to care for whom short-term foster care was not used has already been noted.[20] The teenagers who were placed in short-term foster care were often in care already and unlikely to return home at the end of their placement, even though only two of the 11 placements of 15–17-year-olds lasted longer than three

Table 6

Placement outcome and age of child

	Age in years			
	0–4	*5–9*	*10–14*	*15–17*
Return home	59%	83%	33%	9%
Long-term fostering/adoption	19%	3%	10%	9%
Other temporary care*	8%	6%	14%	55%
Other†	1%	–	5%	18%
Ongoing	13%	8%	38%	9%
	(n=115)	(n=36)	(n=21)	(n=11)

Includes "other short-term foster home" and "residential care"
†*Includes "left care"*

months. Short-term foster care seemed to be merely a staging post, for some, in a long and varied career in care.

Moving on to long-term foster care or adoption was really only a significant outcome for 0–4-year-olds and was the outcome for 22 (19 per cent) placements of this age group. Only four placements of children aged five and over had ended in a placement in a permanent substitute family, and two of these were children returning to their ongoing long-term foster placements after a brief period of respite care. There were at the time of analysis, 27 placements which were still ongoing. Most (19) of them did finally result in a move to a permanent substitute family, but after placements lasting between 9 and 21 months.

This clearly suggests that older children moving on to a permanent substitute home need a longer temporary placement. Caring for and preparing children aged five and over for permanent placement should not really be described as a task of "short-term" foster care. These are really bridging placements of an intermediate length.

The likelihood of a child moving on to another temporary placement also seemed to be related to their age. Less than 10 per cent of the placements of children aged nine years and under, and 14 per cent of 10–14-year-olds, ended in a move to another temporary care placement compared to 55 per cent of the placements of 15–17-year-olds. This would suggest that a large number of placements of 15–17-year-olds were actually ending prematurely; clearly the teenager still needed a temporary care placement yet did not stay in the short-term foster home. Analysis (from the sub-sample) of the social workers' expectations regarding the length of these placements confirmed this. In a number of cases the social worker expected the placement to last longer than six months, longer than a year, or even indefinitely, yet all but two lasted less than three months.

It would appear that the care of 15–17-year-olds is not at present an appropriate task for traditional short-term foster care except in rather exceptional circumstances. An example would be the case of a 15–year-old girl with learning disabilities caring for her baby in her parents' home, for whom short-term foster care provided a respite care placement with her baby while her own mother had a holiday.

Ten to fourteen-year-olds were also slightly more likely to go into another form of temporary care provision than their younger counterparts, and they were the age group most likely to remain in their short-term placement – nearly two-fifths of placements of 10–14-year-olds were ongoing at the time of analysis. Only a third resulted in the child going home. Two young people moved to long-term foster care placements but these were a return to an existing foster home after a respite care break. It would appear that for the majority of children over the age of ten placed in short-term foster care, being in care was unlikely to be a temporary or short-term experience.

Placement outcome and the gender of the child
The gender of the child seemed to have little bearing on placement outcome. Similar numbers of boys and girls went home, or into long-term foster care or adoptive placements; and similar numbers of placements of boys and girls were ongoing. Although a higher percentage of the placements of girls ended in a move to other temporary care, this was probably because it was the most common outcome for 15–17-year-olds, and the outcome for one-sixth of 10–14-year-olds, many of whom were girls. Thus the results suggested that age rather than gender was a more important factor.

Placement outcome and the length of the placement
That the length of the placements was clearly related to outcome is

Table 7

Placement length and outcome of placement

	Return home	Long-term fostering/ adoption	Other temporary care	Other	Ongoing
3 months or less	95%	42%	71%	50%	–
4–6 months	2%	27%	19%	25%	–
7–12 months	2%	31%	10%	25%	59%
Over one year	1%	–	–	–	–
	(n=105)	(n=26)	(n=21)	(n=4)	(n=27)

demonstrated in Table 7. Most significantly, almost all (95 per cent) of the placements resulting in a return home ended in less than three months. Nearly three-quarters of the placements of children who moved into another temporary care placement also ended within three months. However, only 11 placements resulting in long-term fostering or adoption ended within three months, of which seven placements were pre-adoption babies and another two placements were older children returning to their long-term foster family after a respite care break.

Table 8

Placement outcome by legal status at placement

	Voluntary care	In care under orders	Wardship
Return home	65%	35%	24%
Long-term fostering/adoption	10%	17%	47%
Other temporary care	10%	13%	24%
Other	1%	9%	–
Ongoing	14%	26%	6%
	(n=143)	(n=23)	(n=17)

Note: Percentages may not total 100 due to rounding

A more detailed look at the 27 placements which lasted between four and 12 months shows that only two had ended in a straightforward return home. Of these 27 placements, 22 were of 0–4-year-olds, 14 of whom moved on to a permanent substitute family. The remainder mostly moved within the care system.

Placement outcome and the legal status
Children in voluntary care were more likely to return home than children in care under orders, who were more likely to remain longer in short-term foster care or move on to a permanent substitute family.

An overwhelming proportion (90 per cent) of children who went home were in voluntary care, but for the children in voluntary care in the ongoing placements, it would probably be some time before they went home and unlikely that many of them would go home at all.

The pattern for warded children was very different. Nearly half of the placements of children who were wards of court resulted in them going to a permanent substitute family, and almost a quarter in a move to another form of temporary care. Only just under a quarter of the placements of warded children ended in a return home, and only six per cent (just one placement) was ongoing. Thus although warded children seemed less likely to experience a very long "short-term" foster placement (three-quarters of the placements had ended in six months, and at the time of analysis none had lasted over a year), they were less likely to go home. The majority moved to another "in care" placement, which could well be another temporary care situation. These children seemed to be particularly vulnerable to multiple placements, which have been demonstrated to be a hazard of the care system.[21,22]

The use of short-term foster care by the Area Teams
At the time of this survey, field social workers in Newcastle upon Tyne were located in five Area Teams each headed by an Area Director. Each had a main Area office and, where appropriate, sub-offices to cater for specific geographical locations. Area 1 covered the east side of the city and was largely an inner city area with a high density of population housed in older type properties yet with some new and innovative council housing estates which housed a large number of lone parents. Area 4

covered a large part of the west inner city and was largely characterised by older run down areas, some blocks of high rise flats and new and unpopular council housing estates populated by those who had nowhere else to go. Families moved frequently from one address to another and consequently few had settled extended families around them. Area 5 was very similar, covering the rest of the west inner city, but extending much further west into the more suburban areas of the city. Area 2 was, however, quite different and covered the city centre and adjacent suburbs. These suburbs housed a more middle class population and had more expensive housing, and many flats and hotels, but with no new estates with young families. Area 3 lay to the north of this, covering a much wider suburban area, extending almost into the country in furthermost areas and covering villages now encompassed by the city area. It also covered areas of council housing which accommodated families with problems.

The Adoption and Fostering Unit was a centralised team serving all the Area Teams, and was responsible for the recruitment and training of all short-term foster carers. Short-term foster homes were allocated on request from this central unit where a register of all short-term foster carers was kept.

Numbers and distribution within the Area Teams
The demand for public child care provision in the different Area Teams varied considerably. An analysis of the population of children in care in Newcastle upon Tyne on the 31 March 1988 showed that almost three-quarters of the children in care were the responsibility of three Area Teams – Areas 4, 5 and 1 – and it was clear that children in care tended to come from certain parts of the city. There were also differences in the demand for short-term foster care and the following analysis shows some considerable variation in the way the Area Teams used this resource. There was also an unevenness in the demand for placements at different times of the year. The extent to which the offices used this service varied considerably. Area 4 made the most placements, 27 per cent of the total, with Area 5 coming a very close second with 25 per cent. Area 3 made 20 per cent of all placements, and Area 1 made 15 per cent. Area 2 made only four per cent. The bulk of the placements (about half of all

Table 9

Age of children placed by the Area Teams

Age in years	Area 1	Area 2	Area 3	Area 4	Area 5	Others
0–4	71%	75%	51%	71%	49%	81%
5–9	14%	–	35%	25%	13%	6%
10–14	7%	–	5%	–	33%	12%
15–17	7%	25%	8%	4%	4%	–
	(n=28)	(n=8)	(n=37)	(n=49)	(n=45)	(n=16)

Note: Percentages may not total 100 due to rounding

placements) were being made from the west of the city. These figures establish a similarity in the quantity of need for short-term foster care placements in Areas 4 and 5, yet a more detailed analysis of their patterns of use showed that the way in which these areas were using the resource differed in a number of significant ways.

The age of children placed by the different Area Teams
An examination of the ages of the children placed by the Area Teams shows they were using short-term foster homes for different age groups (see Table 9). Further investigation is needed to show if this is the result of differences in child care populations, local patterns of need, or policies operated by the Area Teams themselves. Whether a child of a certain age entered a short-term foster care placement may well have depended on where they lived in the city. An important question is why Area 4 placed 50 per cent more young children than Area 5 when these two teams had a very similar catchment area for children in care. This raises concerns about the equality of service provision and outcome across the authority.

The legal status of children in the different Area Teams
The legal route to care which each of the Area Teams favoured differed across the authority yet this did not appear to be related to the age of the children they were placing. Both Areas 4 and 5 had a very high proportion of children in voluntary care, in spite of the different age profiles they

presented. A much higher proportion of the children placed by Area 1 were in care under orders, and only two-thirds of the children were in voluntary care. Area 3 placed far more children under wardship – nearly a fifth of Area 3's placements were wards of court compared to one-tenth of the whole sample. Area 2, placing children at either end of the age spectrum, made no use of wardship, but had the highest proportion of children in care under orders. Given that legal status has been linked to length of stay in care,[23] it is clear that the Area Teams had different needs for short-term foster care provision.

The length of placements made by different Area Teams

Again, particularly striking differences between Areas 4 and 5 are evident. Four-fifths of Area 4's placements had ended within three months, compared to only just over a half of those made by Area 5. Not one placement made by Area 4 had continued beyond twelve months, but 16 per cent of placements made by Area 5 (most of which were still ongoing at the time of analysis) had lasted over a year. Area 5 made 56 per cent of the placements lasting over a year, with the majority of the remainder being made by Area 1.

The outcome of placements made by different Area Teams

All Area Teams used short-term foster care to provide short stays for very young children to some extent. Areas 3 and 4 were largely using short-term fostering to provide short stays for young children returning home very quickly. Areas 1 and 5 were placing more children who needed longer temporary stays, either in foster care or other forms of temporary care provision. Most of these were young children, especially in Area 1, but some placements made by Area 5 were of young teenagers. Only a small number of placements were of children moving on to permanent substitute care after only a few months in a short-term foster home, and one-third of these were placed by Adoption and Fostering Unit social workers, another third by Area 3, and the remaining third by the other teams together.

Summary of main findings

A large proportion of placements ended very quickly, within three months, but the remaining placements continued for some considerable time. Short-term foster care was predominantly being used for babies and pre-school children. Some of these children remained in short-term foster care for a significant portion of their young lives, but most children in short-term foster care returned home quickly. Most of the children were in voluntary care. Short-term foster homes were also providing placements of varying lengths and functions for children of all ages who might be going to a long-term foster home or to adoptive parents, who might require further assessment, or who needed to remain in temporary care. The study has also shown that different Area Teams were demanding different resources from these foster homes.

Different age groups seemed to experience different lengths of placement – though the association is not straightforward. Ten to fourteen-year-olds were most likely to need a lengthy placement. Placements of 15–17-year-olds frequently ended very quickly and probably prematurely. The *Child Care Now* study[24] also highlighted the difficulties of maintaining placements for this age group. A small number of 0–four-year-olds needed placements of just a few months in order to prepare them for placement with permanent substitute families. The majority of 0–nine-year-olds needed a very short placement before returning home, but a significant number of these children did not return home quickly, and appeared to require very lengthy temporary placements.

References

1 City of Newcastle upon Tyne Social Services, *Report on the Review of Child Care Residential Resources*, 1989.

2 See 1 above.

3 Department of Health, *Children in Care of Local Authorities 1988*, Department of Health, Personal Social Services, Local Authority Statistics, 1988.

4 Rowe J, Hundleby M, and Garnett L, *Child Care Now*, BAAF, 1989.

5 See 3 above.

6 See 4 above.

7   See 3 above.

8   Department of Health and Social Security, *Social Work Decisions in Child Care*, HMSO, 1985.

9   See 4 above.

10 Millham S, Bullock R, Hosie K, and Haak M, *Lost in Care: The problems of maintaining links between children in care and their families*, Gower, 1986.

11 See 10 above.

12 Trasler G, *In Place of Parents: A study of foster care*, Routledge & Kegan Paul, 1960.

13 Parker R A, *Decision in Child Care*, Allen & Unwin, 1966.

14 George V, *Foster Care: Theory and Practice*, Routledge & Kegan Paul, 1970.

15 Berridge D, and Cleaver H, *Foster Home Breakdown*, Blackwell, 1987.

16 Strathclyde Social Services, *Fostering and Adoption Disruption Research Project – the temporary placements*, Scottish Office Central Research Unit Papers, 1988.

17 See 15 above.

18 See 4 above.

19 See 4 above.

20 See 3 above.

21 See 8 above.

22 Department of Health, *Patterns and Outcomes in Child Placement*, HMSO, 1991.

23 See 10 above.

24 See 4 above.

6 Characteristics of the children, their families, and the social work intervention

Aims

This chapter looks in much more detail at the placements and at the children and families who needed them. It examines whether the children (and the families of the children) who experienced short placements of three months or less have characteristics which differ from those of the children who experienced longer placements. It looks at the nature of the social work intervention in each placement and also relates this to the length of the placement. The aim is to identify indicators which might be useful in planning what type of foster care resource a child is likely to need.

Notes on the methodology

The information in this chapter comes from a sub-sample of 104 placements made between February and July 1989 inclusive. Detailed information was obtained about these placements from the children's social workers by means of a questionnaire. In almost all cases the questionnaire was completed by interview. First, information about the child was obtained; then data about the child's home circumstances and birth family; finally, information was sought about the social work involvement in the placement.

Interviewing all the social workers proved very time consuming, but meant that information on all (100 per cent) of the placements was obtained. The social workers were extremely helpful and co-operative, and data is only missing where it was not available to social workers; for example, no information was available about the mother who abandoned her baby and was never traced. The interviews were carried out as soon as possible after the placement of the child, and it was always stressed to social workers that the information sought was that available at the time of the placement.

A problem with obtaining data in this way was the total reliance on social workers' perceptions, which undoubtedly limits the usefulness of the data. Time simply did not permit examination of the social work files, or interviews with children, families or foster carers. Perhaps, though, this was not unrealistic; placement decisions were largely made by social workers on the basis of the information available to them. If that information was inadequate for research purposes then it was also inadequate to guide decisions that affected children's lives: a number of studies have demonstrated that it is the social work input which is often crucial in determining the length of the child's stay in care.[1]

Finally, statistical tests (chi-square)* were carried out to ascertain whether or not there were any significant differences between the prevalence of a variable in the longer and the shorter placements. The small size of the sample has limited the number of tests in which it has been possible to get a valid result. There is also the problem of overlapping variables. Some factors may operate or interact together. Without isolating specific factors by rigorous statistical controls it is not possible to identify them as predictors. Yet some interesting patterns have emerged indicating those variables important in decision making about the type of placement a child is likely to need.

Information about the ethnic origin of the children was obtained on the questionnaire, but the number of placements of black children (nine out of 104) has been too small for separate analysis. However, the provision of short-term foster care for black children deserves attention, and more detail and discussion about these nine placements is included in this chapter.

The characteristics of the children
Many studies have examined the characteristics of foster children with a view to determining whether they have any bearing on the success or failure of the placement.[2,3,4,5] Consensus has generally been hard to

---

*Chi-square is a test of significance of the degree of association between variables. It measures the probability that the variation which occurs can be accounted for by chance (and thus if the results are in fact reflecting real differences). Results were considered to be significant only when the probability of this was 0.05 or less (i.e. when only 5 times in a hundred might the distribution be expected through chance.)

achieve apart from the factor of age. In 1987 Berridge and Cleaver[6] concluded from their study that in seeking to link placement outcome to characteristics of children they discovered few significant indicators. Others have examined whether the characteristics of children have any bearing on whether or not a child is admitted to care, and found that the profiles of admitted and not admitted children and their families looked remarkably alike.[7] It is not surprising, therefore, that the only characteristics found to be significantly different for the children who had short as opposed to those who had longer placements were whether or not they were on the Child Protection Register, legal status, and age.

Disability/long-term illness: Only seven per cent of placements were provided for children with a disability or a long term illness.

Health: In the majority of placements the children were considered to be reasonably healthy. In about a third of the sample the child was considered to have health related problems of a general kind, for example, asthma, failure to thrive and general poor health, and minor problems with vision and/or hearing.

Child abused/on Child Protection Register: Overall, in only a quarter of the placements were the children on the Child Protection Register, though this proportion varies between the age groups.

Children whose placements lasted between four and six months were Elargely pre-school children moving on to permanent placement. As many as two-thirds of these children were on the Child Protection Register compared to only a fifth of those whose placements lasted less than three months, and a quarter of those lasting over six months.

However, when asked if the child had been abused or neglected at any

Table 10

Child protection registration and age of child

Percentage of each age group on Child Protection Register				
	0–4 years	*5–9 years*	*10–14 years*	*15–17 years*
% on CPR	28%	32%	8%	25%

time in their life, even if not currently at risk or on the Register, social workers considered this to be the case in three-fifths of placements. The percentage was remarkably high for children over school age. Nearly nine-tenths of 15–17-year-olds were thought to have been abused or neglected at some time in their lives. Well over four-fifths of 10–14-year-olds and almost the same proportion of five to nine-year-olds were judged to have been abused or neglected. In fact only one child over the age of 10 and only five children between the ages of five and nine years were not thought or known to have been abused or neglected at some time in their lives.

First time in care: In just over half the placements (51 per cent) the child had not been in care previously, but this average masks great variations between the different age groups. Whilst the placement was the first time in care for 70 per cent of 0–4-year-olds, this was the case for only a third of 5–9-year-olds, 15 per cent of 10–14-year-olds, and only 12 per cent of 15–17-year-olds. Older children in short-term foster care did appear to be those who had embarked on their "career" in care when they were younger.

In approximately one-fifth of the placements the children were already in care at the time of the placement. These children were of all ages from very young babies to 17–year-olds, though more than half of them were over 12 years old (in striking contrast to the whole sample where less than one-tenth was over age 12.) The vast majority of these children (14 out of 18 placements) had been received into care because of abuse, neglect, or being abandoned or rejected, and a high proportion had been placed in short-term foster care because of the disruption of a previous placement. This illustrates again how these older children in care experienced multiple moves and how short-term foster care seemed to be just another staging post.

Emotional problems of child: Social workers were asked what problems the children were experiencing at the time of placement, including learning difficulties, emotional problems, and difficulties in relationships with peers or adults. These have been analysed together under the general heading "emotional problems." Some of the children had a whole range of problems, some had difficulties in only one or two areas, and some had no problems at all.

Only a minority of the younger children were thought to have emotional problems, although analysis of the prevalence of emotional problems by age indicates that as children get older the more likely they are to be experiencing emotional problems. Table 11 shows the percentage of children in each age group said to be experiencing specific problems. A relatively small proportion of preschoolers (who made up three-fifths of the sub-sample) were reported to experience each emotional problem; in contrast, children aged ten years and over were more likely than not to have emotional problems.

These percentages reflect the social workers' perceptions of the children's problems, and sometimes the child's parent(s) was thought to have different views, but this was not often. Mostly social workers were making their judgements on what parents had told them, or what they had perceived themselves. It must be acknowledged that social workers' perceptions of children's problems may be limited by the amount and type of contact with the children. Carers, both birth parents and foster carers, may be inclined for a variety of reasons to underplay the

Table 11

Emotional problems of child and age of child

Percentage of placements in which child was considered to be experiencing the problem

	0–4 years	5–9 years	10–14 years	15–17 years
Too dependent/ independent	12%	27%	8%	63%
Withdrawn/aggressive	15%	55%	69%	50%
Problematic relationship with peers/adults	12%	18%	46%	63%
Learning difficulties	20%	32%	77%	50%
Attention seeking	13%	32%	23%	50%
Anxious/sad etc.	25%	41%	85%	75%
Other problem	5%	14%	23%	13%

Table 12

Emotional problems of child and length of placement

Percentage of placements in which child was considered to be experiencing the problem

	0–3 months	*4–6 months*	*7–12 months*
Too dependent/independent	16%	22%	26%
Withdrawn/aggressive	32%	11%	47%
Problematic relationship with peers/adults	22%	0%	26%
Learning difficulties	28%	11%	58%
Attention seeking	25%	11%	11%
Anxious/sad etc.	34%	44%	58%
Other problem	11%	11%	5%

difficulties children may have. These results are valuable in giving an indication of the prevalence of problems in this sample of children, but this would need to be corroborated by objective measurement.

Reliance on social workers' perceptions does not inevitably lead to low estimates of problems. Packman et al[8] also obtained social workers' perceptions to provide estimates of children's behaviour. They found that parents and social workers 'presented an almost identical picture of the extent and nature of behaviour problems'.

Interesting differences in the prevalence of emotional problems were also found when analysed by length of placement. A higher percentage of children in placements lasting over six months were experiencing emotional problems, but this may well be more a function of age than length of placement.

Emotional reactions such as sadness and anxiety were the most common emotional problems in placements of all lengths. This is hardly surprising when one considers that children in care are frequently reacting to difficulties in their previous living situations even before coping with the trauma of the move and separation. This has important implications for the task of fostering which involves helping children to deal with such emotional difficulties. However, the findings indicated that shorter

Table 13

Behaviour problems and age of child

	Percentage in each age group experiencing the problem			
	0–4 years	5–9 years	10–14 years	15–17 years
eating, sleeping, toileting	25%	46%	0%	13%
defiant/compliant	13%	41%	77%	63%
acting out	21%	55%	46%	75%

placements were less likely to be complicated by emotional factors, especially very short placements and those of young children.

Behaviour problems of the child: Similarly, only some of the children were considered to have behaviour difficulties. A quarter had problems with sleeping, eating, toileting, etc; 31 per cent were said to be either overly defiant or overly compliant; and just over a third had behaviour problems of the acting out type: running away, stealing, abusing drugs or alcohol, hyperactivity, and/or premature sexual awareness or behaviour. Behaviour problems were more likely to be experienced by older age groups, except that, predictably, problems of eating, sleeping and toileting were concentrated in the 0–nine-year-olds.

As with emotional problems, the results indicate that whether or not a child has behaviour problems at placement is most likely to be a reflection of their age; they also again suggest that the bulk of short-term foster placements were uncomplicated by problematic behaviour, especially short placements and those of young children. This could have important implications for the organisation of the service and the recruitment of foster carers. Different families in the community have different skills, resources and experiences, and could be selectively recruited for specific groups of children. This could help both with recruitment of more carers, and ensure their suitability for the specific task required of them. For example, foster carers caring for young children for very short periods (for relief or respite care breaks) may not have to have the same level of skill and experience as carers taking older children in more complex situations for longer periods.

Where the child was placed from

On average, two-thirds of the children were living at home immediately prior to the short-term foster placement. The remainder were placed from a variety of other situations, with nearly a fifth from some form of institutional care.

However, as Table 15 shows, there are considerable differences in the numbers of children in each age group placed from home. Around three-quarters of children aged 0–9 years were placed from home and only slightly fewer 10–14-year-olds, but only a quarter of 15–17-year-olds were placed from home. Indeed, around half of all placements from residential care were of teenagers aged 15–17 years.

Table 15 also shows the percentage of children of different ages who had returned home at the time of analysis. It would suggest that a child of nine years or younger has a very high chance of returning home. However, only less than a quarter of children aged ten and over are likely to have returned home within several months of their placement. This corroborates the conclusion from the previous chapter that only a very small number of these children aged ten and over really need a "short" foster care placement for they are relatively unlikely to return home

Table 14

Where the child was placed from

Home	66%
Hospital	14%
Residential care	5%
Short-term foster home	4%
Long-term foster home	2%
Relative	2%
Other	8%
	(n=104)

Note: Percentages may not total 100 due to rounding

Table 15

Percentage of children who came from home and percentage who returned home

	0–4 years	5–9 years	10–14 years	15–17 years
came from home	69%	77%	62%	25%
returned home	59%	77%	23%	13%

quickly. Repeatedly it appears that for most older children short-term foster care was simply a "staging post" in their stay in care, whilst for many younger children it was a very brief stay away from home. The needs of the two groups of children must therefore be very different and the organisation of the service, and the recruitment and training of foster carers should take this into account.

Children of all ages were placed from other "in care" situations, but they made up only two per cent of 0–four-year-olds and about a sixth of five to nine-year-olds, in contrast to a third of 10–14-year-olds and nearly two-fifths of 15–17-year-olds. This is consistent with the finding that a high proportion of children over 12 years old were already in the care system at the time of placement.

A child placed from home was most likely to have a short placement. Table 16 compares the length of placements of children placed from home, hospital, and residential care. It was shown in the previous chapter that all children who had returned home at the time of analysis had a short placement (none lasted longer than four months). Of the children who were placed from home it is those who were unable to return home quickly who were likely to have very lengthy temporary placement, for approximately half the placements from home lasting longer than three months were still ongoing at the time of analysis. Children placed from home are likely to need only a short placement (less than three months), unless there are indicators that a return home may be problematic, in which case they are most likely to need a long temporary placement.

Half of the children placed from hospital were pre-adoption babies, who were mostly placed for adoption within three months. Overall,

Table 16

Where child placed from and length of placement

	Home	*Residential care*	*Hospital*
3 months or less	80%	60%	50%
4–6 months	4%	–	36%
7–12 months	16%	40%	14%
	(n=69)	(n=5)	(n=14)

children placed from hospital did not seem to have very lengthy placements, and in just over half of the few placements lasting between four and six months the children were placed from hospital.

Birth family composition

Millham et al[9] and Packman et al[10] described the families of children coming into care as 'chaotic, and rapidly changing households' and 'fragmented and complex families' respectively. Consequently this study not only sought information about the children's birth parents, but also ascertained who had been the child's main caretakers prior to their entry into the care system, i.e. when they were last living at home.

Only just under a quarter of the placements were of children whose main caretakers were their two original parents (as compared to around 78 per cent of all British children aged under 16 years in 1985).[11] The overwhelming majority (58 per cent) were living with either their birth mother (54 per cent) or their birth father (four per cent) alone (compared in 1987 to a figure of 14 per cent of all families with dependent children).[12] A further 11 per cent were living with their birth mother and either a stepfather, a cohabitee, or another relative. Children from all different home situations were equally likely to experience short or longer placements. A further seven per cent were babies placed direct from hospital for adoption, who had never been cared for at home.

What is very striking is that only about a quarter (27 per cent) of the children were being cared for by their birth father before their entry into the care system. Fifteen to 17-year-olds were the only group equally likely to have come from the care of both their birth parents, as from the care of a single parent. All other age groups were most likely to come from a single parent family, especially 10–14-year-olds, of whom 77 per cent came from a single parent family. Millham et al[13] found that in 41 per cent of cases the child's birth father was living in the household at the time of the child's entry into the care system. However, 45 per cent of Millham's sample were over the age of 13 years. It would appear that fathers could be a very under-utilised resource in the care of these children. The new concept of "parental responsibility" in the Children Act 1989 aims to encourage both parents to participate in the child's upbringing,[14] and fathers to take a more active role in the care of their offspring.

Some 40 per cent of the placements in this sample were of children placed in short-term care as part of a sibling group, which compares with the figure of 45 per cent found by Millham et al.[15] Eleven sibling pairs were placed together in short-term foster homes. There were four groups of three siblings (though it was not always possible to place these together) and one family of seven children (placed in a number of different foster homes). Children from larger sibling groups in short-term foster care were likely to be separated from brothers and sisters as well as from their parents.

Rutter[16] noted that separation from siblings can compound the stress experienced by children separated from their parents. In 1987, Berridge and Cleaver[17] found that long-term foster placements where sibling groups were placed together were more successful, and one year later Thoburn and Rowe[18] also found that sibling placements broke down less often. Wedge and Mantle[19] reported in 1991 a study of sibling groups referred for permanent placement, where they found that the impact of siblings could in fact work against placement stability as well as for it, depending on the situation. They looked at reasons for splitting or not splitting sibling groups. As so many sibling groups were placed in short-term foster care placements, and that decisions about keeping the children together should be taken very carefully, homes should be recruited to ensure that brothers and sisters can be kept together, both to reduce the stress for the children and to try to prevent unnecessary further family disintegration.

Contact

Earlier studies[20,21] had already stressed the importance of access (now contact) if a child was to return home following admission to care. In 1986, Millham et al[22] particularly emphasised the special need for access for children in "limbo" situations, and indeed their need for wider links with friends, extended family and their own familiar territory (all of which is included in the concept of "contact" introduced by the Children Act 1989) in order to ease the impact of separation upon the child. In their follow-up study on access disputes,[23] Millham et al confirmed that withering links with home affect many children in care, and identified two kinds of barriers: specific restrictions affecting around a third of children in care (pre-1989 Act terminology), and non-specific restrictions – difficulties inherent in placements, such as hostility, distance and inaccessibility – affecting as many as two-thirds of children in care.

This study was only able to ask about plans for access, and was not able to monitor what actually took place. There were plans for access in most placements. In only 15 per cent of placements were there no plans for the child to have access visits to their birth family, and this was often because of the short period of the placement, though in some cases the child had been abandoned or rejected by birth parents. Access was planned even when there were no immediate plans for rehabilitation, and often access visits were seen as an important opportunity to achieve some specific tasks in regard to the parent–child relationship. The purpose of many access visits was simply to ease rehabilitation (38 per cent), although in 28 per cent it was to maintain links: in 20 per cent of placements whilst plans were made, and in eight per cent where no rehabilitation was planned. In only three per cent of placements was access specifically for the purpose of severing contact between parent and child, that is, to say goodbye.

Mother's agreement with social work plan

Conflict over the social work plan, though it did not seem to occur often with the sample in this study (most of the children, it will be remembered were in voluntary care), seemed to be related to the child experiencing a longer temporary placement. In nearly three-quarters of placements the child's mother was said to be in agreement with the social work plan.

Four-fifths of these placements (58 per cent of the total) lasted three months or less. In contrast, of the one-tenth of placements where the mother was said to disagree with the plan, only a third ended in three months or less. In a further tenth, the mother was thought to be unsure, and two-thirds of these ended in three months or less.

Mother's commitment to the child's return home

Whether or not the mother wanted her child back was an important factor in the length of a child's placement. In 55 per cent of the placements the child's mother was said to be committed to her child's return to her care, and over four-fifths of these were placements lasting three months or less. In about a third of the cases, the social worker reported that the mother did not want her child home and only just under a half of these ended within three months. In the 12 per cent of placements where the mother was unsure, nine-tenths were short.

Father's agreement with social work plan

In only 27 per cent of the placements was the birth father present at home prior to the children's entry into the care system. In a high percentage of placements the father's agreement to the plan was not applicable (46 per cent) and in a further 15 per cent there was no information about the father's wishes or feelings. About a quarter of the fathers (29) were considered to be in agreement with the social work plan (11 of them had actually been caring for the child before the latter entered care), and 12 per cent were considered not to be in agreement.

In contrast to the findings about the mother's agreement, it is the placements where fathers were *not* in agreement with the plan which were the most likely to last three months or less (but some of these were short because the child moved on to another temporary placement). This is consistent with the earlier finding that it is the fathers of older teenage girls who are most likely to have been involved in the care of the child prior to reception into care and though many of these girls had a short placement this did not denote a return home.

Where the fathers were positive about the planning, placements were less likely to be short. A closer look at these 29 placements shows that where father and mother were both in agreement the placements were indeed short. The lengthy placements were where father agreed and mother disagreed, or where both parents were rejecting the child, or where a change of plan after placement had led to subsequent disagreement. The study suggested that conflict and rejection were often associated with longer stays in care.

Father's commitment to the child's return home

In a number (39 per cent) of placements it would not have been appropriate for the father to resume the care of the child, and the question of his commitment to the child's return was simply not applicable, and no information about the father's wishes was available in a further 15 per cent. Just over a quarter of the fathers were considered not to want the child to return to their care, so in only 15 per cent of the placements was the father judged to be actively committed to the return home of his child.

We have noted that far fewer birth fathers seem to have played an active role in the lives of children in care than birth mothers. What these results clearly suggested was that even fewer were likely to want to be involved in looking after their child once the child had been in care. This is consistent with the findings of Rutter[24] in 1981 regarding 'the adverse effects of separation on the parent–child relationship', and of Packman et al[25] who reported in 1986 'there is a faint suggestion that removal to care may more often exacerbate father–child relationships'.

Problems experienced by the child's birth family

These children in short-term foster care came from families with a range of problems. Parents with their own relationship difficulties and little support from extended family were experiencing health, income and housing problems, so it is perhaps hardly surprising that the stresses and strains of child care became too much for them.

According to the social workers, problems in family relationships were widespread. The majority (65 per cent) of families had problems caring for the child placed, and 46 per cent had difficulties in their relationship with the child. Fifty-five per cent of families were experiencing problems caring for another child in the family. As many as 84 per cent of parents were experiencing relationship problems with spouses or partners (although this was given as the main reason for the placement in only two placements), and four-fifths were experiencing problems with their extended family, or had no extended family in the area. Additionally, one-third were experiencing housing problems, two-thirds had income problems, and 43 per cent had health problems. Only 18 per cent were thought to abuse drugs or alcohol, and two-fifths had other family problems.

Unfortunately, these estimates do not record the families' own views, but rely on social workers' perceptions, and what has been reported to them, rather than on first hand experience. Nevertheless, this may not detract significantly from the accuracy of the evidence. Packman et al[26] were able to compare social workers' perceptions of the families' problems in their sample with the families' own perception of their problems, and found that 'on a sizable number of issues the two views were in reasonably close accord, and occasionally the high degree of consensus came as a surprise to us'. On the other hand, Fisher et al[27] found that social workers and birth families tended to see problems from different perspectives, with families seeing the problems as being in "people" whilst the social workers saw problems in the "relationships".

These figures painted a picture of many families with multiple problems to face, and children growing up surrounded by difficulty, disharmony and emotional upheaval. The study stressed how significantly relationship problems – between parent and child, between mothers and their friends, partners or husbands, and within the extended family – figured in the lives of these families. It is likely that it was family relationships which took the strain in the stressful situations of unemployment, poverty, poor housing, and poor health. Rutter concluded in 1981 from his studies of parent–child interaction that 'the wider social environment does have an impact on parenting behaviour'.[28] Certainly, Millham et al found the same family characteristics: 'It is clear that many children who come into care will have experienced severe family dislocations. Their family structures are fragile with frequent marital conflicts, cohabitations and changes of accommodation.'[29]

Family problems seemed fairly evenly spread across all age groups. Certain problems were more common in the families of the younger children, and others in the families of older children, but families of

Table 17

Birth families' problems and length of placement

Percentage of placements where family was experiencing the problem

	0–3 months	*4–6 months*	*7–12 months*
Care of this child	58%	75%	90%
Care of other child	53%	50%	68%
Relationship with child	42%	50%	63%
Marital/relationship problems	87%	75%	79%
Extended family	80%	63%	90%
Housing	34%	63%	37%
Income	63%	63%	79%
Health	49%	25%	26%
Drugs/alcohol	20%	38%	5%
Other	38%	38%	53%

children in all age groups were experiencing problems of one sort or another, many coping with several problems at once.

It was the families of the children needing the longest placements who were the most likely to be experiencing problems. As many as 90 per cent of them were said to have problems caring for the child in placement and/or with their extended family. Nearly four fifths had marital/relationship problems, and a similar proportion had income problems. Two-thirds had relationship problems with the child in placement and/or problems caring for another child in the family. Half of them had other problems, and a third had housing problems. It is perhaps surprising that only a quarter were thought to have problems with their health, and only five per cent were said to abuse drugs or alcohol.

In the shorter placements (lasting 0–3 months) the most frequent problems were marital and relationship problems, and problems with the extended family. It is in these placements that the families were most likely to have health problems, and two thirds had income problems. Over half of these families also had problems caring for the child in placement and for other children in the family.

Although the children in placements lasting 4–6 months seemed to experience fewer problems themselves, this was not the case for their families. The most frequent problems for the families of these children appeared to be problems caring for the child in placement and marital/relationship problems. It is these families who experienced the most problems with housing and with abuse of drugs or alcohol, and three-fifths of them had problems with their extended family and/or income. However they were the least likely to have health problems.

It became clear from the analysis that the majority of these families were coping with a whole range of problems and difficulties. It is not surprising to then find, in the next section, that many children were in short-term foster care because of their family circumstances.

The reason for placement

Two studies in the 1980s, by Packman et al[30] and by the National Children's Bureau (NCB)[31] found that, in general, children were admitted to care for reasons that were many and various. They found it necessary to differentiate on the basis of reason for admission. The NCB study separated interventions 'offering a service to the family by temporarily relieving the family of the child' (family service) from those based on 'the need to intervene in the family and rescue the child' (rescue) and 'the problem behaviour of some children and the need in some way to control it'. Packman named these three groups of children "volunteered", "victims", and "villains".[32]

Two of the NCB categories – family service and rescue – have been used to group the reasons for placement given in this study. None of the reasons given in this sample corresponded to the NCB's third theme.

Social workers were asked to say what they considered to be the most important reason for this particular placement. In 50 per cent of placements it was because the parent(s) was experiencing difficulties and needed help. Thus the placements were made first and foremost to assist a parent, not to rescue or control a child. For further analysis these placements were grouped together under the heading "service to families". Most frequently the parents could not cope with the child and needed help; a variety of reasons made them feel inadequate for, or overwhelmed by, the task of parenting a child. Sixteen placements were made for this reason. Fourteen placements were made because a parent was ill or in hospital, and a further 13 because the parent had other problems and was unable to provide for the child. In just two placements were marital problems thought to be the main reason for the placement, and a further two were because of the parents' imprisonment or arrest. Five placements were respite care placements made specifically to allow birth parents or foster carers to go away on holiday.

A further 34 per cent of placements were made to rescue children from harmful or potentially harmful situations, and these were grouped together under the heading "intervention". Thirteen placements were made because the child was abandoned or rejected, and another 13 because the child had been neglected or was at risk of neglect. Five placements were made because a child had been abused or was at risk, and three because of poor home conditions.

The reason for placement was significantly related to the length of the placement. Nearly nine-tenths of the placements that have been defined as "service to families" lasted three months or less, compared to just half of the placements where the reason was "intervention".

In no placement was the child's own behaviour given as the main reason for the placement, though some of the children did have behaviour or emotional problems. Parents who were unable to cope did complain that their children's behaviour was unmanageable, but often social workers considered the behaviour was not inappropriate for the child's age or that the behaviour was the result of, not the cause of, inadequate parenting. Fisher et al[33] noted in 1986 that it was frequently a seemingly trivial event that precipitated children into care, but an event that, coming on top of many difficulties, constituted for the parents the "last straw".

On the evidence of the social workers then, these children were placed in short-term foster homes largely because their families were experiencing problems. It would have been interesting to have investigated what the *children* considered to be the reasons for their placements, and whether they had been helped to understand their apparent blamelessness in the situation. It is quite possible that the children considered themselves being punished for some misdemeanour. As was evidenced in the crisis that occurred over child sexual abuse in Cleveland in 1987, taking children into care as a solution for family problems could often cause children to become "double victims" – they suffer from their home situations and suffer admission to care.[34]

A number of placements were made for other reasons. Six placements were of babies going for adoption (one abandoned baby is included below in this group of pre-adoptive babies though the initial reason for the placement was to provide care whilst the baby's mother was sought); three placements were of pregnant teenage girls needing help and support before and after the birth of their babies; and one further placement was of a teenage girl requesting care herself because of relationship difficulties with her mother and her mother's cohabitee. One of the placements made for "other reasons" was made because a father was refusing to allow a teenage girl to return home. Possibly, this is another case of rejection, though the teenager was described as "largely out of control" and "a particularly difficult teenager", therefore the reasons were more complicated. Six placements were made because of disruptions of previous placements. These results are summarised in Table 18.

The purpose of the placement
It would be true to say that the purpose of all the short-term placements was to provide temporary care for the child. However, over and above that, the aim could be further differentiated, largely in relation to the overall social work plan for the child. In 37 per cent of all cases the purpose was the rehabilitation of the child, with a further 13 per cent placed for respite care (a single short break to provide parents with relief, not a regular arrangement). Thus, in half of the placements the aim was to provide care until the child returned home. Approximately one-fifth of placements were for the purpose of assessment, and in 13 per cent of placements the purpose was to seek a permanent placement for the child, although six per cent were pre-adoptive placements of newborn babies.

The remaining 20 placements had aims more difficult to categorise: three were to allow a period of adjustment following a breakdown; four were for the protection of the child; four were unusual respite care placements; and three were to provide temporary care awaiting another resource. The remaining six were placements of teenagers, of which the aim in four cases was preparation for independent living – three of these

Table 18

Reason for placement

		Per cent
A)	"Service to families"	50
	Parent ill	14
	Parent has other problems*	16
	Parent unable to cope with child	15
	Parent requesting respite care	5
B)	"Intervention"	34
	Rejected/abandoned	13
	State of home	3
	Neglected or at risk	13
	Abused or at risk	5
C)	Pre-adoptive	6
D)	Disruption of previous placement	6
E)	Provide assistance for teenager	5
		(n=104)

*Including marital problems and imprisonment/arrest
Note: Percentages may not total 100 due to rounding*

girls were also pregnant; in one it was to provide an experience of family life; and in the other, to help the teenager with relationship problems.

There was an identifiable relationship between the purpose of the placement and its length, as can be clearly seen in Table 19, particularly in respect of those placements where the purpose was to return the child home. Where the purpose of placement was rehabilitation or respite care the vast majority (94 per cent) ended within three months. Similarly, where the purpose was to provide a bridge to independence the placements only lasted up to three months, but these placements were of teenage girls and largely ended prematurely. Only half of the placements where the aim was adoption or long-term fostering lasted less than three months and it is likely that these were the pre-adoption babies who were traditionally placed with adopters within six weeks. The other placements

Table 19

Purpose of placement analysed by length

	Return home	Assessment	Long-term fostering/ adoption	Other
3 months or less	94%	39%	46%	77%
4–6 months	–	17%	15%	18%
7–12 months	6%	43%	39%	6%
	(n=51)	(n=23)	(n=13)	(n=17)

where the purpose was permanent placement had already lasted, as was shown in the previous chapter, anything up to 12 months. Placements where the purpose was assessment were least likely to end within three months.

The plan for the child

In most cases the purpose of the placement was linked to the overall social work plan for the child, so the data in relation to plans is consistent with the data on the purpose of the placements. In just over half of the placements the plan for the child was rehabilitation with a birth parent (with an additional two per cent returning to established long-term foster placements). In 11 per cent of the placements the plan was adoption and, in four per cent, long-term fostering. In five per cent of placements the plan was for the young person to move to independent living. However, in about a fifth of all placements there was no clear plan at all for the child at the time of placement (or the plan was another assessment placement).

In the previous chapter it was clearly shown that outcome is related to length of placement, but this does not help in predicting placement length unless the outcomes correspond to the plan at the time of placement. Table 20 attempts overall to relate plan to outcome, though it is only able to compare percentages and does not show if the plan corresponded to outcome in individual placements. Return home is actually the outcome in almost the same percentage of placements as it was the plan, and the

Table 20

Plan in relation to outcome

	Plan	*Outcome*
Return home	54%	55%
Long-term fostering/adoption	14%	13%
Residential care	1%	8%
Independence	5%	1%
Other	5%	2%
Short-term foster care	0%	7%
No plan	21%	–
Ongoing	–	15%
	(n=104)	(n=104)

same is true of permanent placement. This is not the case, however, for residential care which was the planned outcome in only one per cent of placements, but was the actual outcome in eight per cent; or for independence, which was the outcome in only one per cent* of placements whilst it was the plan for five per cent.

Social workers' predictions of placement length
Social workers were asked to say how long they had expected the placement to last at the time of placement. They appeared honestly to judge their expectations at the time of placement and were asked to refer to planning documents that had been completed at the time of placement or very shortly afterwards.

Social workers predicted that about two-thirds of placements would end within three months, and they were accurate in 92 per cent of these cases. In fact, as Table 23 demonstrates, more placements ended in three months (73 per cent) than were expected (68 per cent), four of which had been expected to end in four to six months, three of which had been

---

*Even in this one case, the outcome was recorded as "independence" because that young person had reached the age of 18 years, not necessarily because she had achieved a measure of maturity or independence in psychological terms to ensure successful independent living.

Table 21

Comparison of predicted lengths and actual lengths of placements

	ACTUAL LENGTH		PREDICTED LENGTH	
	Per cent	*Cumulative Per cent*	*Per cent*	*Cumulative Per cent*
3 months or less	68%	68%	73%	73%
4–6 months	15%	84%	9%	82%
7–12 months	5%	89%	ended 3%	85%
			ongoing 15%	100%
over one year	1%	90%		
indefinite	11%	100%		

expected to end in 7–12 months, and one which had been planned to last over a year. We have already seen that several of the placements that were planned to last longer were of teenage girls. Only eight per cent of placements predicted to last three months or less in fact lasted longer.

In percentage terms, social workers' predictions were therefore fairly consistent with actual outcome. Millham et al also found that, broadly speaking, social workers' expectations regarding children's length of stay in care were fairly accurate, and concluded from an earlier study[35] that expectations were a strong determinant of outcome.

Ongoing court involvement; court order being sought

In the vast majority of placements there was no current active legal involvement – in only 13 per cent of placements was a court order being sought, and two thirds of these placements had ended in six months. A court order was being sought in 67 per cent of placements lasting four to six months, but we have already seen that few of these children returned home (Chapter 5).

Previous involvement with social services

In nine-tenths of placements the child was already known to social services, and in 79 per cent there was an open case file. This suggested that in most cases social workers did have information about the child and their family before the short-term placement. This should allow a measure of planning, but only two-fifths of placements were planned, and three-fifths of placements were categorised by social workers as emergency placements. A number of other studies have commented on the high proportion of emergency admissions to care. As Rowe et al remark:

'"Emergency" is a word used rather loosely in social services departments. One is reminded of the social worker who said she was expecting to do an emergency placement in three weeks' time.'[36]

More seriously, though, the studies by Rowe et al,[37] Millham et al,[38] and Packman et al[39] all note the deleterious effect of unplanned admissions on the experience of placement for both the children and their families and remind us that movements between placements can also be emergencies.

Significant differences in shorter and longer placements

This study has confirmed that the placements of children in short-term foster homes were either very short (three months or less) or, with only a few exceptions, lasted very much longer. The results were analysed statistically to ascertain whether or not there were any differences at placement between the characteristics of the children who had short placements and those of the children who had longer placements; which variables, if any, could be useful in predicting the length of placement a child is likely to need; which differences could have occurred just by chance. The chi-square test was applied to the data on the computer and the results showed that the occurrence of a number of variables did appear to be significantly different.*

Variables which were related to the circumstances of the placement and the nature of the social work plan were equally, if not more, significant than individual characteristics of the child and family. The child's legal status, the reason for the placement, the purpose of the

---

*A larger sample would undoubtedly have given more reliable results on the more marginal variables. These results are intended for general guidance only.

placement, the plan for the child, and ongoing involvement with the courts, all appeared to be important variables in determining the placement length.

Where the child was on the Child Protection Register, and where the family had problems caring for the child, this was related to a child experiencing a longer placement. The child was significantly more likely to have a short placement where there were health problems, where the birth mother agreed with the social work plan and/or was committed to the child's return home. The last two reasons would suggest that conflict and rejection are significant indicators of the likelihood of a lengthy placement.

Under the Foster Placement (Children) Regulations 1991 the authority responsible for placing a child with a foster carer must now be satisfied that the 'placement with the particular foster parent is the most suitable placement having regard to all the circumstances' (5.(1)(b)), except in emergency and immediate placements and then only for 24 hours (11.(1)). It should be possible, in spite of the apparent urgency of many short-term placements, to make informed choices about the most suitable placement for a child. Many social workers make these judgements intuitively, though it requires experience and knowledge to do so. The above analysis does not seek to replace professional judgement, but to provide additional tools for the job, and help avoid creating both further difficulties for already vulnerable children, and also unnecessary stress for foster carers unprepared for specific tasks.

Race, religion, language and culture

Information was obtained in the questionnaire on the race and religion of the children in the sub-sample. Of the 104 placements studied nine were of black and minority ethnic children, about 8.5 per cent of the sample. The number was too small to analyse statistically but a closer look at these placements is useful in addressing some of the issues raised in Chapter 1 in relation to the needs of black children and their families in the provision of short-term foster care.

An estimate of the minority ethnic population in Newcastle upon Tyne resident in private households between 1986 and 1988[40] (just before this study was undertaken) suggests it was around 3.6 per cent of the total population. The largest single ethnic groups were Pakistani and Bangladeshi. Only a relatively small proportion were from mixed ethnic backgrounds (approximately 0.2 per cent). Consequently, there was a higher proportion of short-term foster placements of black and minority ethnic children than would be expected on the basis of population. Chapter 1 showed that this is very much the national picture.

The differences between different ethnic groups found in major studies is also reflected in these short-term foster placements. *Child Care Now*[41] found that Asian children were underrepresented in all age groups in the mid 1980s, and that children from mixed parentage were considerably overrepresented. Bebbington and Miles[42] found that a child of mixed parentage is two and a half times more likely to be admitted to care, particularly among pre-schoolers. The findings from this study were very similar. Of this small sub-sample only two per cent (two of the nine placements of racially different children) were of children of Asian origin, and the other seven were all of children of mixed parentage. Five of the nine placements were of children whose home was in the geographical area of just one Area Team.

The shortest of these placements lasted just four days. Six lasted three months or less. One of these was a pre-adoption placement of a newborn baby. The other five children returned quickly to the care of their birth mother, though in one case this was in a special family unit of a general hospital. Four of these children were in voluntary care, and two were wards of court (but in one, care and control was given to the mother). The other three placements lasted nine months, 14 months and 19 months. Two were in voluntary care, the third a ward of court, and all moved to permanent substitute families at the end of their placement. The proportion of warded children was much higher than in the sample generally.

The proportion of single parents was also much greater. Only one child lived with both birth parents together prior to placement, and one was a single mother placing a newborn baby for adoption. All of the children of mixed parentage came from single parent families headed by their mother. Juliet Cheetham[43] has drawn attention to the particular difficulties faced by single white mothers caring for mixed parentage children (see Chapter 1). Not all these mothers were white, however. One mother of two of the children was herself from a mixed white/African-Caribbean background, and another was South-east Asian (Filipino). It is certainly the case that problems of income, housing and/or health (both physical and mental) were said to be facing most of these families. Stress and breakdown in mental health was a factor in three placements.

In Chapter 1, lack of extended family support was given as one reason for the overrepresentation of black children in care. Absence of extended family, rejection by them or lack of adequate support from them were noted as a factor in the need for six out of these nine placements. Cultural expectations within the extended family were a reason for placement for at least two of the children. These factors highlight the issue of whether or not there were services available which were relevant and adequate to the needs of the minority ethnic communities, and whether there was adequate knowledge of support networks within the communities.

The diversity of ethnic backgrounds of the children in these nine placements is striking: there were children whose heritage included Asian, West African, African-Caribbean, North African, South-east Asian and British ethnic origins. Legislation and government guidance is clear that the services provided must now take this diversity into account. Social workers must therefore learn what is important for the people with whom they work by careful observation, by listening, and by asking their consumers.[44] Social work practice must reflect multiracial society by taking account of its diversity and providing a pool of foster carers suitable to the needs of all the racial groups in the area.

The family structures to which the children belonged were, with the exception of one two-parent family, all immensely complex and diverse. Four of the children had full or half siblings already adopted by another family. A brother and sister were placed together in short-term care, but left an older half brother at home, and had another older half sibling living permanently elsewhere with relatives. One child had an older half sister living permanently with another parent. A boy whose placement finally resulted in his being adopted had two white half brothers: one of them was already in long-term care separately, the other was initially placed with him in this short-term placement but returned home after a very short time.

How far did the foster placements provided in this study match the needs of the children and their families in relation to race, religion, language and culture, bearing in mind that the placements were all made before the implementation of the Children Act 1989? Given the diversity of these children and their families what is particularly striking is the homogeneity of the foster families in which they were placed. All the children were placed in white families, consisting of a married couple with their birth children. In some families the older children had moved away, in some there were other (white) short-term foster children. In only three placements were the foster carers known to be of the same religion as the child, but in another three the child's religion had not been recorded. All the foster homes were in residential areas close to the city and easily accessible by public transport, but only two placements were made specifically in the geographical area covered by the Area Team in which the child and family were living.

The placements of the two Asian children are each illustrative of difficulties that can arise in transracial short-term foster placements of black children (see Chapter 1 for discussion). In the six week long placement of a six month old baby girl following her mother's hospitalisation, contact was maintained by the foster carer taking the baby into hospital to see her mother. There were concerns about the patterns of the baby's feeding and about the level at which she was being stimulated. The foster carer was asked to advise and help the baby's mother with these two concerns, but without special training she could only have been able to do this from a white cultural perspective, and must have had difficulties communicating with the baby's mother who did not speak English. The social worker stated that she would have preferred a foster family of the same race, or a hospital placement that would have allowed the baby to stay with her mother. It was indeed possible to provide this after six weeks and the baby moved into a special family unit with her mother.

In the other placement, a 20–month-old boy was in short-term foster care awaiting adoption. The situation must have required particular sensitivity and understanding to meet the needs of the child and to support his (unmarried) mother, as the boy had been rejected by his family "on cultural grounds", placed (illegally) privately by his mother in an adoptive placement, which was said to have broken down after two weeks, due to the mother's visits, and resulted in this short-term foster placement. The plan was for a same race (Asian) adoptive placement to be found, but the child spent 14 months of his formative years with a white family, before being placed for adoption just before his third birthday.

The efforts of the social workers and foster carers and the resilience of children and their families hopefully prevented these circumstances adversely affecting the outcomes for these individual children. Nonetheless, if the children are representative, and if the aims of the Children Act 1989 are genuinely to be met, the findings from these nine placements suggest that significant changes may need to be made in both policy and practice in relation to the provision of services, including short-term foster care, to black children in need and their families.

Summary of main findings

The study confirmed that short-term foster care was still largely a resource for very young children, many of whom had not been in care before, and who went home very quickly. Most were reasonably healthy, with few emotional and behaviour problems, but in many cases their families needed help to maintain a consistent standard of parenting in the face of multiple social problems. Mostly the children needed a very short stay in care to provide a break for their families (many of whom were single mothers overwhelmed by difficulties and lacked support from an extended family).

Short-term foster care performed a number of different functions. Although for the majority of younger children it was just a brief stay before returning home, we find repeatedly that for a child of 10 years or more, it was simply a "staging post" in their "career" in the care system. Older children were more likely to have emotional and behaviour problems, and more likely to have been in care before. For a small number it was a bridge to a permanent substitute family. These groups of children must have very different needs and the organisation of the service, and the recruitment and training of foster carers should take this into account.

Statistical tests suggested that it was those variables which are related to the circumstances of the placement and the nature of the social work plan which were most significant in determining the length of placement a child was likely to need. The characteristics of the children themselves and their families did not adequately account for differences in the length of the placements.

It is true to say that many of the short-term placements in this study were made quickly at very short notice. However, many of the children were already known to the Social Services, and this should have allowed a greater measure of planning. It should not be assumed that the matching of the child to the foster carers, and preparation of both child and foster carers, are unimportant when a placement is "short-term".[45] Furthermore, the importance of matching becomes even more apparent when it is remembered that a substantial number of these placements, some of very young children, were far from being short and would more appropriately be called "temporary" or "bridging" placements.

This study suggests that if better planning is to enable more appropriate matching of child to foster carer, it could be both useful and possible to separate the different functions of short-term foster care in order to recruit and prepare carers for the needs of children, and to recruit them to provide different types of foster care, according to the demand, and the location of the children and families requiring the service.

References

1 For discussion see Millham S, Bullock R, Hosie K, and Haak M, *Lost in Care: The problems of maintaining links between children in care and their families*, Gower, 1986.

2 Trasler G, *In Place of Parents: A study of foster care*, Routledge & Kegan Paul, 1960.

3 Parker R A, *Decision in Child Care*, Allen & Unwin, 1966.

4 George V, *Foster Care: Theory and Practice*, Routledge & Kegan Paul, 1970.

5 Berridge D, and Cleaver H, *Foster Home Breakdown*, Blackwell, 1987.

6 See 5 above.

7 Packman J, Randall J, and Jacques N, *Who Needs Care? Social work decisions about children*, Blackwell, 1986.

8 See 7 above.

9 See 1 above.

10 See 7 above.

11 Kiernan K, and Wicks M, *Family Change and Future Policy*, Joseph Rowntree, 1990.

12 See 11 above.

13 See 1 above.

14 Department of Health, *Introduction to the Children Act 1989*, HMSO, 1989.

15 See 1 above.

16 Rutter M, *Maternal Deprivation Reassessed*, (1st and 2nd edns) Penguin Books, 1972, 1981.

17 See 5 above.

18 Thoburn J, and Rowe J, 'Research: A snapshot of permanent family placement', *Adoption & Fostering*, 12:3, 1988.

19 Wedge P, and Mantle G, *Sibling Groups and Social Work*, Avebury, 1991.

20 Fanshel D, and Shinn E B, *Children in Foster Care: A longitudinal investigation*, Columbia University Press, 1978, USA.

21 Aldgate J, 'Identification of factors influencing children's length of stay in care' in J Triseliotis (ed), *New Developments in Foster Care and Adoption*, Routledge & Kegan Paul, 1980.

22 See 1 above.

23 Millham S, Bullock R, Hosie K, and Little M, *Access Disputes in Child Care*, Gower, 1989.

24 See 16 above.

25 See 7 above.

26 See 7 above.

27 Fisher M, Marsh P, and Phillips D with Sainsbury E, *In and Out of Care*, BAAF/Batsford, 1986.

28 See 16 above.

29 See 1 above.

30 See 7 above.

31 Vernon J, and Fruin D, *In Care: A Study of Social Work Decision Making*, National Children's Bureau, 1986.

32 Department of Health & Social Security, *Social Work Decisions in Child Care*, HMSO, 1985.

33 See 27 above.

34 House of Commons, *Report of the Inquiry into Child Abuse in Cleveland in 1987*, Cm. 412, HMSO, 1988.

35 Dartington Social Research Unit, Predicting Children's Length of Stay in Care and the Relevance of Family Links, Research Report, 1984.

36 Rowe J, Hundleby M, and Garnett L, *Child Care Now*, BAAF, 1989.

37 See 36 above.

38 See 1 above.

39 See 7 above.

40 Haskey J, 'The ethnic minority populations resident in private households – estimates by county and metropolitan district of England and Wales', *Population Trends*, No. 63, Spring 1991.

41 See 36 above.

42 Bebbington A, and Miles J, 'The background of children who enter local authority care', *British Journal of Social Work*, 19:5, 1989.

43 Cheetham J (ed), *Social Work and Ethnicity*, Allen & Unwin, 1982.

44 Caesar G, Parchment M, and Berridge D, *Black Perspectives on Services for Children in Need*, NCB/Barnardo's, 1994. In this study feedback was specifically obtained from black and minority ethnic users about the services offered under study.

45 Triseliotis J, 'Foster care outcomes: a review of key research findings', *Adoption & Fostering*, 13:3, 1989.

7 Conclusions and implications for policy and practice

Short-term fostering is playing an increasingly significant part in public child care provision. Towards the end of the 1980s it has been estimated that it provided services for over two-fifths of children placed in foster care each year,[1] and provided the first placement experience for around one third of children entering the care system.[2] However, the trend towards a greater number of short placements appears to be continuing today, and they now form an important and growing proportion of the child care workload of social services departments.

Short-term fostering first emerged as a service largely to meet the needs of parents unable to look after their children during a period of illness, confinement, or similar short-term difficulty, but now provides a range of placements of varying length, performing different functions for children of all ages and of different legal status. The substantial majority of these placements are indeed very short, but the remainder can last considerably longer and would perhaps more appropriately be designated "temporary" or "intermediate".

From the time of the Children Act 1948, fostering was seen as the placement of first choice, but even though the Curtis Report[3] already identified at that time the large number of admissions that were short-stay, it was only in the early 1950s that foster care was also recognised as the best method for short-term care. From 1948 the proportion of children fostered rose to a peak of 52 per cent of all children in care in 1963.[4] Part of this was due to the immense pressure of applications for temporary reception into care, and the general expansion of short-term care. As early as 1957 the report by Gray and Parr[5] identified a distinction between short and long-term foster carers in that some would take just one child for a number of years, whilst others would take a succession of children for short periods. The demarcation line between short and long placements was fixed at eight weeks in the 1955 Boarding Out

Regulations, but was thought to be around six months in the period following the Children Act 1975, when the differences between short (or temporary) placements and long (or permanent) placements became more clearly distinguished.[6] With the implementation of the Children Act 1989, there has been a move away from these rigid distinctions based on arbitrary time scales, towards the aim of tailoring placements more to the needs of individual children.

Developments in attachment theory and permanency theory led to a belief in the 1970s and early 1980s that even short breaks could damage the child's relationship with his or her psychological parent, and temporary substitute care was considered very much a last resort, and one which could be detrimental to the development especially of very young children. Attention was directed at the achievement of permanency and adoption, and away from the imaginative and supportive use of short-term foster care.

However, in spite of these earlier fears that any separation experience might be harmful to young and vulnerable children, later research studies pointed to the positive use of short-term foster care, in providing temporary care for children in emergencies or at short notice. For example, the large scale survey of placements of children provided by the *Child Care Now* study[7] showed that 'the day to day, bread and butter work of fostering is still the placement of young children needing care for a brief period during a family crisis or to give relief to their hard-pressed parents.' Packman et al[8] showed that care was very much a part of the lives of children who, for the most part, remained with their families. It was acknowledged that short episodes of foster care could be perceived as helpful rather than as a last resort, and could play a significant part in preventing family breakdown. It was suggested that the family stresses that lead to the need for accommodation often arise quickly and are resolved quickly, so that rather than avoiding the separation of children from their families at all costs, an alternative would be to put in place a comprehensive set of social work practices and procedures designed to restore children quickly to their parents.[9]

The untapped potential of medium and short-term placements for the relief of families under stress, and for the treatment of many child and family problems was acknowledged, and in the mid 1980s the idea of using short-term care as a preventive measure to avoid permanent breakdown by offering temporary relief was explored.[10,11]

Chapter 4 looked at how attachments develop and bonds are formed, as well as the effects of separation and how these can be minimised. By taking account of these processes and the significance of continuity, the trauma of separation in fostering situations can be reduced. Separation need not mean discontinuity, provided that children, parents and carers are properly prepared for the children leaving and returning home. If foster care provides familiar circumstances for children while they are out of their home environment, in localities close to their own homes, in a way that can supplement the care of the birth families rather than supplant them, it can play a role in helping the child's whole family. Important factors include pre-placement visits, familiar objects and patterns of care, and careful preparation of parents, children and carers so that they understand normal reactions to separation. In addition an appropriate level of contact with parents and other family members whilst the child is in placement, and placing brothers and sisters together as far as possible are helpful. These are the first significant steps in bringing about the child's eventual reunion with their family.

It has been reported that birth parents can feel ambivalent at the time of separation and placement, and growing understanding of this has helped define the need for social work with the parents of children in care at times of separation, and in providing them with support at the time of reunion. Acceptance of the use of multiple caretakers makes new approaches to shared care viable, and by including and supporting parents and working in partnership with them they need not relinquish their parental responsibility to gain access to the service.

The results of the study
This study showed that short-term foster care was still largely a resource for very young children, many of whom had not previously been in the care system, and who returned home very quickly. Sixty-three per cent of the children were four years old and under, and 83 per cent were under ten. Half the children had not been in care before. Most of the children were reasonably healthy, one third were considered to have a health problem and only seven per cent had a disability or long-term

illness. The bulk of the placements, especially short placements, were uncomplicated by behavioural or emotional problems. Three-fifths of the placements resulted in the child's return home, and 95 per cent of these placements lasted three months or less. The children only needed a very short stay in care largely to provide a break for their families, many of whom (54 per cent) were single mothers who became overwhelmed by difficulties. Overall, one third of families were experiencing housing problems, and 43 per cent had health problems. Problems in family relationships were widespread: 84 per cent had relationship problems with spouses or partners; 46 per cent had difficulties in their relationship with the child; and four-fifths lacked support from an extended family.

Over and above this the study revealed that short-term foster care provided for more complex patterns of need and use for children of different age groups and different legal status. One quarter of the children were on the Child Protection Register, and 34 per cent of the placements involved an element of protection or rescue. Only one 15–17-year-old and only a third of 10–14-year-olds had returned home within six months. Older children (ten years and over) were more likely to have a wide range of emotional and behavioural problems.

A significant minority of the placements lasted well over a year, and some even longer. It is apparent that differences in the length of the placements were far from being explained by differences in the children themselves, or in their families, but were more dependent on the nature of the social work intervention with the family at the time. Statistical tests suggested that it was those variables which were related to the circumstances of the placement and the nature of the social work plan which were most significantly related to the length of placement a child was likely to need. Social work plans and expectations for the child were instrumental in determining the need for and use of short-term foster care, and patterns of use varied from one social work team to another.

The children in this study who were placed in short-term foster homes largely because their families were experiencing problems mostly returned home very quickly. A Dartington study[12] of factors affecting children's length of stay in care makes this pertinent point:

'If so many children are able to leave care quickly, the question might be raised as to whether any of them might have been kept out of care in the first place and whether or not there are differences in policies surrounding the admission of children to care in different local authorities and field social work teams.'[13]

The Children Act 1989 offers the opportunity to provide short-term accommodation as a preventive service to families without the requirement to seek a care order. However, it stresses that accommodation should be offered to the families of children in need as part of a range of support services which local authorities are empowered to provide under Part III of the Act, and which could reduce the need for children to experience separation from their families. However, while in the future it may be possible to reduce the need for short-term foster care, social workers involved in this study considered it to be a very necessary service. It was in most cases specifically the resource they were seeking for the child, and they would not have preferred an alternative solution, even if one had been available. Three-fifths of the placements were categorised as emergencies, where placement of the child seemed to be the only viable option, even though there was an open case file on four-fifths of the children prior to this placement.

Information about where each child moved to at the end of the placement helped to show how short-term fostering fitted into the wider process of being in the care system, and clearly this was different for different age groups. For the majority of 0–9-year-olds, but for only a very few teenagers, it was a brief stay before they returned home. For some 0–4-year-olds it was a period of temporary care prior to a move to a permanent substitute home. For some 0–9-year-olds, and most 10–14-year-olds, it was a lengthy period of temporary care whilst they were able neither to return home, nor to move on to a permanent alternative placement. Many 15–17-year-olds had only short placements before they moved on, usually earlier than intended, to another form of temporary care. Repeatedly the findings suggested that for most older children short-term foster care was simply a "staging post" in their stay in care. These groups of children are likely to have very different needs and different experiences of short-term foster care. This study suggests that the organisation of the service, and the recruitment and training of foster carers should take this into account.

The data for this study was collected prior to the implementation of the Children Act 1989, but the findings are still relevant today. A recent examination of the children and families using accommodation following the implementation of the Children Act 1989 by Packman et al at the University of Bristol for the Department of Health, and as yet unpublished,[14] reveals many points of similarity between the characteristics of the children and families in the two studies. It confirms the continuing preponderance of short admissions for children accommodated voluntarily, four out of five of whom were fostered, and is evidence that the characteristics of children and families needing these placements has changed little over time.

Key issues for consideration

That so many of the children in this sample experiencing long temporary placements were of pre-school age is particularly worrying, and the implications of lengthy placements for this age group need special consideration. Services need to recognise children's need to form relationships and attachments even whilst plans for their future are being made. It also appears to take a long time to provide permanent substitute placements for children over the age of five years. The provision of specialist intermediate or "bridging" placements for these children needs to be examined.

The needs of black children and their families for short-term foster care provision deserves further study and attention. The requirements of the Children Act 1989 could create the impetus to make the changes needed to provide appropriate and equal short-term foster care services for black children. Requirements under the Children Act 1989 are to consult the consumers themselves, to publicise arrangements to receive representations and complaints, and to monitor family support services under Part III.

Barnardo's and The National Children's Bureau have recently collaborated to research black perspectives on services for children in need.[15] They offer a number of solutions to the pressing concern about social service provision for black children. They stress it is important to ensure short-term foster care services are specifically relevant to and adequate for the needs of minority ethnic groups – taking into account the specific cultural, physical, emotional, and religious needs of children – by recruiting substitute families who can respond to the cultural needs of ethnic minority children and to their experience of discrimination. They recommend that an agency strategy is needed to ensure the framework of service delivery is based on an anti-racist approach; and that black people are involved at all levels of service delivery and monitoring, decentralising services where possible. They emphasise the importance of recording ethnic origin and using this information to aid future planning.

In this study short-term foster care did not provide a viable resource for most teenagers who needed accommodation or care. The provision of short-term fostering for teenagers needs to be examined further in the light of the increasing proportion of adolescents entering the care system at the same time that residential provision is largely being curtailed.[16]

It must be asked why the Area Teams were using short-term fostering in such different ways. It is not clear from this study if it was because of the different populations they served, or different policies and practices, or indeed a combination of reasons. It would be fruitful to examine further why these differences in practice exist in order to know more about what influences the demand for and use of a service.

Some children seem to be the victims of conflict – both within their own families, and between their family and outside agencies —and this was associated with longer stays in short-term foster placements. This underlines the importance of finding positive ways of working in partnership with families, which is a philosophy underpinning the Children Act 1989, and of offering training to social workers in skills of counselling, advocacy, conciliation and negotiation.

Finally, the study has highlighted how few birth fathers play a role in the lives of children in short-term foster care. Sixty per cent of these fathers were not involved in the decision to place their child in care, and only around a quarter of the children were living at home with their fathers prior to admission to care. What is more, the admission to care was likely to reduce the number of fathers playing an active part even further. We need to know why this occurs and how fathers can be encouraged to contribute positively to the welfare of their children.

A differentiated model for short-term foster care services

The Children Act 1989 presents social services departments with new challenges and opportunities to provide more imaginative services for the children they are "looking after", in ways that will positively promote their welfare and prevent family disintegration. In this study a number of broad patterns have emerged, which may be useful pointers in identifying the type of services that could be usefully developed to meet the aims of the new Act. Short-term family placement is not a single unified service and hopefully the information in this study will assist in planning and reorganising fostering services in a way more appropriate to the many and various needs of children.

I would like to suggest a new model for re-organising short-term fostering services to reflect the complex patterns of need for temporary care demonstrated by the findings of this study. I would suggest that broadly there are four different types of need for temporary care provision.

i)   Babies and young children aged 0–4 years, including pre-adoptive babies, where the plan at placement is that they should be placed with a permanent substitute family

It is usually clear that these children will not return home; they are as often as not in some form of legal care and it seems they need a temporary placement of up to about nine months in order to place them in a permanent substitute family, usually for adoption. The demand for this service is likely to be relatively small and uneven, and social work expertise could be built up in a centrally based service to provide specialist experience in handling, for example, the legal systems, arrangements for contact, and requirements arising from race, religion, language, culture, long-term illness and disability.

ii)   Children aged 0–9 years needing short placements of up to three months

This service would largely be for children who are placed from home and return home very quickly, usually to assist a parent (in the overwhelming majority of cases their mother) over a difficult patch for a very short time. As there is a high level of need for this service it is likely to be very important, and in this study formed about 60 percent of all short-term placements. The need and demand for this service, however, could vary greatly, possibly depending on the features of the local community, and policies of social work teams. It could form part of a preventive "package" of services to families, provided on a basis of partnership with families, for in the majority of these short placements the parents were in agreement with the social work plan and committed to their child's return. It would be best developed on a geographical basis so that children can remain as close as possible to their familiar communities. These children will mostly be children in need for whom "accommodation" can be provided on a voluntary basis under the Children Act 1989. The service could supplement other respite care provision for children in need. This study suggests that short-term foster care is a resource that could continue to provide for single short breaks of respite care which are unlikely to last longer than three months, and might be provided alongside services which allow for regular, planned episodes of respite care which can now be more simply arranged under the Children Act 1989, both for children with disabilities as well as other children in need.

iii) Children aged 0–9 years needing longer temporary care
Often there is no immediate clear plan for these children, and assessment is required before plans can be made and implemented. A higher degree of conflict over the plan is likely between parents and the social services departments, and the children may not be able to return home for some time, perhaps because of rejection by their parents or the need to safeguard their welfare. Possibly, though by no means mostly, there is legal involvement.

The results of this study indicated that these children frequently remain in the limbo of a short-term placement for over a year and possibly over two years. They may well need a placement with a permanent substitute family at the end of that time. The likelihood that bonds may form between the child and the family needs to be considered when a child is placed to minimise the need for the child to suffer being painfully uprooted again. However, children may experience a number of moves during the placement, for example, moving to assessment facilities or home on trial, before returning to foster care, preferably with the same carers. An aim would be to minimise the moves these vulnerable children suffer. The service will not be required for large numbers of children, but carers will benefit from being experienced, and from the provision of extra training and support to cope with the problems that can arise from meeting children's emotional needs in a climate of uncertainty; from the special requirements of black and minority ethnic children from diverse cultural backgrounds; and in helping children who may have suffered trauma, abuse or neglect in their own homes.

iv)   Young people aged 10 years and over
Although there is undoubtedly a need to be able to place children of this age group in foster homes at short notice, the study shows that children of this age needing foster care are most likely to need a longer foster placement (except in exceptional circumstances such as a respite care break), and are less likely to return home. The evidence of this study is that most of these teenagers are going to be in care for some time, and they need a placement to provide them with care and parenting over a lengthy period. However, permanence in substitute care is difficult to achieve for this age group who seem most at risk of multiple moves within the care system.

Maintaining placements and avoiding breakdown is a major task. Many of the few short-term placements of 15–17 year olds in this sample broke down very quickly. Foster carers for these children need special training and support, although the teenagers in short-term foster care may be atypical of the majority of young people in care, in that they are rarely in care because of their own behaviour (although their own behaviour may indeed be problematic), but rather because of a failure of parenting, and atypical in that they are predominantly girls. A suitable fostering resource to meet the needs of teenagers for emergency family placement needs to be developed.

A framework such as this could help define more explicitly and accurately at the outset the aim, purpose and duration of a child's short-term foster placement. It would enable aims and objectives to be agreed with children, birth parents and foster carers, and misunderstandings and disagreements to be cleared up at the outset. It would help all concerned to understand more clearly the nature of the separation experience for both children and parents, and the nature and level of involvement of birth parents. The framework could also help in ensuring appropriate preparation, training and remuneration of foster carers, by clarifying their tasks, roles and functions. Finally it could assist in planning and locating fostering resources.

The Children Act 1989 – positively accommodating children

Under the Children Act 1989 accommodation is now to be seen as a service to provide positive support to children in need and their families. What emerges very clearly from this study is the potential to develop short-term fostering as a very positive family support service, providing accommodation under s.20 of the Act.

The concept of respite care allows parents to place their children for short breaks while retaining prime responsibility for them. An analysis by Stephen Webb[17] has shown that it can be crisis-driven (used on an emergency basis as a temporary stop gap provision which provides a period of immediate relief for both parents and children) or contingency-driven (based on the idea of prevention and conceived as part of a planned package of care resources).

Short-term foster care could be used to provide both crisis-driven and contingency-driven relief care. This study demonstrates that there are many families for whom single short episodes of accommodation would be important in tiding them over a current crisis. Indeed, providing short-term relief care for families of young children has emerged from these findings as still being a significant and clearly distinguishable service provided by short-term foster homes often on the basis of agreement, with a clear plan for a speedy return home to which all parties are committed.

However, the potential demonstrated by this study needs to be developed further if it is genuinely to meet the requirements of the Children Act 1989. A separate service needs to be designed to reduce the stigma currently attached to local authority care – a service that is no longer associated with other services which aim to rescue, assess or treat children and families. It needs to reduce the fear of loss of parental control by clearly acknowledging that parents retain full responsibility and by being sensitive to the requirements of race, religion, language and culture. To truly work in partnership, parents need to be consulted about the choice of placement from a pool of local placements. Children need to be helped to keep in touch with important people and other aspects of their lives, while being offered positive alternative experiences that many children are given through informal respite arrangements.

The study reminds us that families suffer from a multiplicity of stresses. Providing relief by sharing the burden of child care for families who lack informal respite facilities is a positive initiative which can help parents and perhaps reduce the levels of difficulty and disharmony in which many of these children are growing up.

References

1 Triseliotis J, 'Foster care outcomes: a review of key research findings', *Adoption & Fostering*, 13:3, 1989.

2 Millham S, Bullock R, Hosie K, and Haak M, *Lost in Care: The problems of maintaining links between children in care and their families*, Gower, 1986.

3 Home Office, *Report of the Care of Children Committee* (Curtis Report), Cm 6922, HMSO, 1946.

4 Packman J, *The Child's Generation* (2nd edn), Blackwell/Robertson, 1981.

5 Gray P G, and Parr E A, *Children in Care and the Recruitment of Foster Parents*, COI, The Social Survey, 1957.

6 Shaw M, and Lebens K, 'Children between families', *Adoption and Fostering*, 84, no 2 of 1976.

7 Rowe J, Hundleby M, and Garnett L, *Child Care Now*, BAAF, 1989.

8 Packman J, Randall J, and Jacques N, *Who Needs Care? Social work decisions about children*, Blackwell, 1986.

9 Thorpe D, and Bilson A, 'The Leaving Care Curve', *Community Care*, 22 October 1987.

10 Department of Health & Social Security, *Social Work Decisions in Child Care*, HMSO, 1985.

11 Department of Health & Social Security, *Review of Child Care Law*, HMSO, 1985.

12 Fisher M, Marsh P, and Phillips D with Sainsbury E, *In and out of care*, BAAF/Batsford, 1986.

13 Dartington Social Research Unit, *Predicting Children's Length of Stay in Care and the Relevance of Family Links*, Research Report, 1984.

14 Packman J, *Accommodation: The implementation of Section 20*, Dartington Research Unit, Report to the Department of Health, 1994.

15 Caesar G, Parchment M, and Berridge D, *Black Perspectives on Services for Children in Need*, National Children's Bureau/Barnardo's, 1994.

16 Bullock R, 'The implications of recent child care research findings for foster care', *Adoption & Fostering*, 14:3, 1990.

17 For a full description of this model of respite care devised by Stephen Webb see Webb S, 'Preventing reception into care; a literature review of respite care', *Adoption & Fostering*, 14:2, 1990.

Further reading

Adamson G, *The Caretakers*, Bookstall Publications, 1972.

Adcock M, and White R (eds), *Terminating Parental Contact*, ABAFA, 1980.

Ahmed S, Cheetham J, and Small J, *Social Work with Black Children and their Families*, BAAF/Batsford, 1986.

Aldgate J, 'Identification of factors influencing children's length of stay in care' in J Triseliotis (ed), *New Developments in Foster Care and Adoption*, Routledge & Kegan Paul, 1980.

Aldgate J, 'Work with children experiencing separation and loss: A theoretical framework', in Aldgate J and Simmonds J, *Direct Work with Children*, BAAF/Batsford, 1988.

Aldgate J, Pratt R, and Duggan M, 'Using care away from home to prevent family breakdown', *Adoption & Fostering*, 13:2, 1989.

Aldgate J, 'Attachment theory and its application to child care social work – an introduction', in Lishman J (ed), *Handbook of Theory for Practice Teachers in Social Work*, Jessica Kinglsey, 1991.

Aldgate J, 'Respite care for children – an old remedy in a new package', in Marsh P, and Triseliotis J, *Prevention and Reuinification in Child Care*, BAAF/Batsford, 1993.

Audit Commission, *Seen but not Heard*, HMSO, 1994.

BAAF, 'A comprehensive adoption service for London', BAAF, 1982.

Banks N, 'Techniques for direct identity work with black children', *Adoption & Fostering*, 16:3, 1992.

BASW, *Guidelines for Practice in Family Placement*, BASW, 1982.

Bebbington A, and Miles J, 'The background of children who enter local authority care', *British Journal of Social Work*, 19:5, 1989.

Berridge D, and Cleaver H, *Foster Home Breakdown*, Blackwell, 1987.

Bowlby J, *Maternal Care and Mental Health*, World Health Organisation, 1951.

Bowlby J, *Child Care and the Growth of Love* (1st & 2nd edns), Penguin Books, 1953, 1965.

Bowlby J, *Attachment and Loss: Volume 1, Attachment*, Penguin Books, 1969.

Bowlby J, *Attachment and Loss: Volume 2, Separation*, Penguin Books, 1973.

Bowlby J, *The Making and Breaking of Affectional Bonds*, Tavistock Publications, 1979.

Bradshaw J, *Child Poverty and Deprivation in the UK*, National Children's Bureau, 1990.

Bullock R, 'The implications of recent child care research findings for foster care', *Adoption & Fostering*, 14:3, 1990.

Caesar G, Parchment M, and Berridge D, *Black Perspectives on Services for Children in Need*, NCB/Barnardo's, 1994.

Cann W, 'Meeting the needs of the Asian community', *Adoption & Fostering*, 8:1, 1984.

Cheetham J, James W, Loney M, Mayer B, and Prescott W (eds), *Social and Community Work in a Multiracial Society*, Harper & Row/Open University Press, 1981.

Cheetham J (ed), *Social Work and Ethnicity*, Allen & Unwin, 1982.

City of Newcastle upon Tyne Social Services, *Report on the Review of Child Care Residential Resources*, 1989.

Clarke A, and Clarke A, *Early Experience: Myth and Evidence*, Open Books, 1976.

Cooper J D, *Patterns of Family Placement*, National Children's Bureau, 1978.

Dartington Social Research Unit, *Predicting Children's Length of Stay in Care and the Relevance of Family Links*, Research Report, 1984.

Department of Health & Social Security, *Report of the Committee of Inquiry into the Care and Supervision provided in relation to Maria Colwell*, HMSO, 1974.

Department of Health & Social Security, *Foster Care – A guide to practice*, HMSO, 1976.

Department of Health & Social Security, *Social Work Decisions in Child Care*, HMSO, 1985.

Department of Health & Social Security, *Review of Child Care Law*, HMSO, 1985.

Department of Health & Social Security, *The Law on Child Care and Family Services*, Cm 62, HMSO, 1987.

Department of Health, *Children in Care of Local Authorities 1988*, Department of Health, Personal Social Services, Local Authority Statistics, 1988.

Department of Health, *Introduction to the Children Act 1989*, HMSO, 1989.

Department of Health, *The Care of Children: Principles and Practice in Regulations and Guidance*, HMSO, 1989.

Department of Health, *Review of Adoption Law: Report to ministers of an inter-departmental working group*, 1990.

Department of Health, *Patterns and outcomes in child placement: messages from current research and their implications*, HMSO, 1991.

Department of Heatlh, *The Children Act 1989 Guidance and Regulations Volume 3 Family Placements*, HMSO, 1991.

Department of Health/Welsh Office/Home Office/Lord Chancellor's Department, *Adoption: The Future*, Cm 2288, HMSO, 1993.

Department of Health, *The Challenge of Partnership in Child Protection*, HMSO, 1995.

Fahlberg V, *A Child's Journey through Placement*, BAAF, 1994.

Fanshel D, and Shinn E B, *Children in Foster Care: A longitudinal investigation*, Columbia University Press, 1978, USA.

Fisher M, Marsh P, and Phillips D with Sainsbury E, *In and Out of Care*, BAAF/Batsford, 1986.

Freud A, and Dann S, 'An experiment in group upbringing', *Psychoanal. Stud. Child.*, vol 6, 1951.

George V, *Foster Care: Theory and practice*, Routledge & Kegan Paul, 1970.

Goldstein J, Freud A, and Solnit A J, *Beyond the Best Interests of the Child*, The Free Press: MacMillan, 1973, USA.

Gray P G, and Parr E A, *Children in Care and the Recruitment of Foster Parents*, COI, The Social Survey, 1957.

Hall D, and Stacey M, *Beyond Separation*, Routledge & Kegan Paul, 1979.

Hammond C, 'BAAF and the placement needs of children from minority ethnic groups', *Adoption & Fostering*, 14:1, 1990.

Haskey J, 'The ethnic minority populations resident in private households – estimates by county and metropolitan district of England and Wales', *Population Trends*, No. 63, Spring 1991.

Heinecke C, and Westheimer I, *Brief Separations*, Longmans, 1965.

Hess P, 'Parent-child attachment concept: crucial for permanence planning', *Social Casework*, 63:1, 1982, USA.

Hitchman J, *The King of The Barbareens*, Penguin Books, 1960.

Holman R, *Trading in Children*, Routledge & Kegan Paul, 1973.

Holman R, *Inequality in Child Care*, Child Poverty Action Group, 1976.

Holman R, 'Exclusive and inclusive concepts of fostering', in Triseliotis J (ed), *New Developments in Foster Care and Adoption*, Routledge & Kegan Paul, 1980.

Home Office, *Report of the Care of Children Committee*, (Curtis Report), Cm 6922, HMSO, 1946.

House of Commons, *Report of the Inquiry into Child Abuse in Cleveland in 1987*, Cm. 412, HMSO, 1988.

House of Commons, *Children in Care* (Short Report), Social Services Select Committee Report, HMSO, 1984.

Hussell C, and Monaghan B, 'Child care planning in Lambeth', *Adoption & Fostering*, 6:2, 1982.

Jenkins R, 'Long term fostering', *Case Conference*, 15:9, 1969.

Jenkins S, and Norman E, *Filial Deprivation and Foster Care*, Columbia University Press, 1972, USA.

Jenkins S, 'The tie that bonds', in Maluccio A, and Sinanoglu P (eds), *The Challenge of Partnership: Working with parents of children in foster care*, Child Welfare League of America, 1981, USA.

Jordan W, 'Prevention', *Adoption and Fostering*, 105, 1981.

Kiernan K, and Wicks M, *Family Change and Future Policy*, Joseph Rowntree, 1990.

Kufeldt K, 'Temporary foster care', *British Journal of Social Work*, 9:1, 1979.

Lahti J, and Dvorak J, 'Coming home from foster care', in Maluccio A, and Sinanoglu P (eds), *The Challenge of Partnership: Working with parents of children in foster care*, Child Welfare League of America, 1981, USA.

Maas H, and Engler R, *Children in Need of Parents*, Columbia University Press, 1959, USA.

Macdonald S, *All Equal Under the Act*, Race Equality Unit (REU) Personal Social Services, 1991.

Maluccio A N, Fein E, and Olmstead K A, *Permanency Planning for Children: Concepts and methods*, Tavistock, 1986.

Millham S, Bullock R, Hosie K, and Haak M, *Lost in Care: The problems of maintaining links between children in care and their families*, Gower, 1986.
Millham S, Bullock R, Hosie K, and Little M, *Access Disputes in Child Care*, Gower, 1989.

Millham S, Bullock R, and Little M, *Going Home*, Dartmouth, 1993.

Morris C, *The Permanency Principle in Child Care Social Work*, Social Work Monograph 21, University of East Anglia, Norwich, 1984.

Packman J, *The Child's Generation* (2nd edn), Blackwell/Robertson, 1981.

Packman J, Randall J, and Jacques N, *Who Needs Care? Social work decisions about children*, Blackwell, 1986.

Parker R A, *Decision in Child Care*, Allen & Unwin, 1966.

Parker R A (ed), *Caring for Separated Children*, Macmillan, 1980.

Rapoport R, Fogarty M, and Rapoport R N (eds), *Families in Britain*, Routledge & Kegan Paul, 1982.

Robertson J, and Robertson J, 'The Psychological Parent', *Adoption & Fostering*, 87:1, 1977.

Rowe J, and Lambert L, *Children who Wait*, ABAA, 1973.

Rowe J, 'Fostering in the 1970s and beyond', ABAFA. Reprinted in Triseliotis J (ed), *New Developments in Foster Care and Adoption*, Routlede & Kegan Paul, 1980.

Rowe J, *Fostering in the Eighties*, BAAF, 1983.

Rowe J, Hundleby M, and Garnett L, *Child Care Now*, BAAF, 1989.

Rutter M, *Maternal Deprivation Reassessed* (1st and 2nd edns), Penguin Books, 1972, 1981.

Schaffer H R, and Schaffer E B, *Child Care and the Family*, Occasional Papers on Social Administration, No. 25, 1968.

Shaw M, and Lebens K, 'Children between families', *Adoption & Fostering*, 84, no 2 of 1976.

Shaw M, and Hipgrave T, *Specialist Fostering*, BAAF/Batsford, 1983.

Smith P M, and Berridge D, *Ethnicity and Childcare Placements*, National Children's Bureau, 1993.

Social Services Inspectorate, 'Issues of race and culture in the family placement of children', Letter to Directors of Social Services, CI(90)2, Department of Health, 1990.

Solnit A J, 'Least harmful to children', *Adoption & Fostering*, 87, 1977.

Stevenson O, *Someone Else's Child*, Routledge & Kegan Paul, 1965.

Stevenson O, 'Family problems and pattern in the 1980s', *Adoption & Fostering*, 4:2, 1980.

Strathclyde Social Services, *Fostering and Adoption Disruption Research Project, the temporary placements*, Scottish Office Central Research Unit Papers, 1988.

Thoburn J, Murdoch A, and O'Brian A, *Permanence in Child Care*, Blackwell, 1986.

Thoburn J, and Rowe J, 'Research: a snapshot of permanent family placement', *Adoption & Fostering*, 12:3, 1988.

Thoburn J, *Child Placement: Principles and Practice*, Wildwood House/Gower, 1988.

Thoburn J, *Success and Failure in Permanent Family Placement*, Avebury/Gower, 1990.

Thorpe D, 'Career patterns in child care – implications for service', *British Journal of Social Work*, 18:2, 1987.

Thorpe D, and Bilson A, 'The Leaving Care Curve', *Community Care*, 22 October 1987.

Thorpe R, 'The social and psychological situation of the long-term foster child with regard to his natural parents', unpublished PhD Thesis, University of Nottingham, 1974.

Timms N, *Casework in the Child Care Service* (2nd edn), Butterworths, 1969.

Tizard B, and Hodges J, 'Research: Ex-institutional children: a follow-up study to age 16', *Adoption & Fostering*, 14:1, 1990.

Trasler G, *In Place of Parents: A study of foster care*, Routledge & Kegan Paul, 1960.

Triseliotis J (ed), *New Developments in Foster Care and Adoption*, Routledge & Kegan Paul, 1980.

Triseliotis J, 'Identity and security in adoption and long-term fostering', *Adoption & Fostering*, 7:1, 1983.

Triseliotis J, 'Foster care outcomes: a review of key research findings', *Adoption & Fostering*, 13:3, 1989.

Triseliotis J, *Foster Care Outcomes*, NCB Highlight, No.96, 1990.

Vernon J, and Fruin D, *In Care: A Study of Social Work Decision Making*, National Children's Bureau, 1986.

Wallerstein J, and Kelly J, *Surviving the Breakup*, Basic Books, 1980.

Webb S, 'Preventing reception into care: a literature review of respite care', *Adoption & Fostering*, 14:2, 1990.

Wedge P, and Mantle G, *Sibling Groups and Social Work*, Avebury, 1991.

Westacott J, *Bridge to Calmer Waters – A study of a Bridge Families Scheme*, Barnardo's, 1988.

Wolkind S, and Rutter M, 'Children who have been "in care" – an epidemiological study', *Journal of Child Psychiatry and Psychology*, 14, 1973.

Statutes and statutory instruments

Poor Law (Amendment) Act 1834

Children and Young Persons Act 1933

Public Health Act 1936

Children Act 1948

Boarding-out of Children Regulations 1955

Children and Young Persons Act 1963

Children and Young Persons Act 1969

Local Authority Social Services Act 1970

Children Act 1975

Child Care Act 1980

Boarding out of Children (Foster Placement) Regulations 1988

Children Act 1989

Foster Placement (Children) Regulations 1991

Glossary of legal terms
used under Children Act 1989 and under previous legislation

Children Act 1989

Previous legislation

Accommodation

Local Authorities are required to provide *accommodation* for children in need who require it under s.20 of the Act. The acceptance of accommodation is entirely *voluntary*, and the local authority may not continue to provide accommodation for a child under 16 against the wishes of the person or persons with parental responsibility.

Other children accommodated by a local authority may be subject to *care orders*. Both groups are described as being *"looked after"* by the local authority.

Those who are *accommodated* but not *in care* include
- children accommodated under s.20
- children subject to Emergency Protection Orders
- children on remand.

"In care" means subject to a care order (or an interim care order) under s.31. These provisions enable the court to authorise interventions by a local authority where a child would otherwise be significantly at risk. A court may make a care or supervision order if it is satisfied
a)   that the child concerned is suffering, or is likely to suffer, significant harm, and
b)   that the harm, or likelihood of harm, is attributable to
   (1) the care given to the child, or likely to be given to him (or her) if the order were not made, not being what is would be reasonable to expect a parent to give him (or her); or
   (2) the child's being beyond parental control.

Admission to local authority care

All children admitted to local authority care were deemed to be *"in care"*.

"Reception into care"

Children could be "received into care" under the Child Care Act 1980, s.2. These provisions were designed to protect children whose parents could not look after them themselves, or make alternative suitable private provision. Reception into care under this section was often called *voluntary care* because the local authority had no right to keep the child if the parent wished to have him or her back home. However, where a child had been in care for six months or more the parent was required to give 28 days notice of their wish to have the child back.

"Parental rights resolutions"

Where a child had been received into care the local authority Social Services Committee could pass a resolution in which it took over under S.3 of the Child Care Act 1980 the parental rights and duties in respect of a child.

"Committal to care"

A care order (under the Children and Young Persons Act 1969) committed the child to the care of the local authority. Responsibility for the child passed to the local authority which then had parental rights. There were a number of other Acts under which children could be committed to the care of a local authority, for example in wardship, or divorce, or other matrimonial proceedings.

Children Act 1989

Foster placements

The Foster Placement (Children) Regulations 1991 replace the Boarding-out of Children (Foster Placement) Regulations 1988. They apply to the placements of children by local authorities and voluntary organisations with foster carers.

Child in need

In s.17, Part III of the Children Act – means a child who

a)   Is unlikely to achieve or maintain, or to have the opportunity of achieving or maintaining, a reasonable standard of health or development without the provision for him of services by a local authority. . . or whose

b)   health or development is likely to be significantly impaired, or further impaired, without the provision for him of such services. . . or who

c)   is disabled.

Contact

The local authority has a duty (Schedule 2, para 15) to endeavour to promote contact between children it is looking after and their parents, relatives, friends, and other people connected with them, so far as is practicable and consistent with the children's welfare.

Although *contact orders* (s.8, s.34) are similar to access orders, which they replace, the form of the order is different in that rather than provide for the parent to have access to the child, it provides for the child to visit or stay with the person named in the order. "Contact" is used in the widest sense to include both face-to-face contact and keeping in touch by correspondence or telephone calls.

Emergency procedures

The *Emergency Protection Order* (s.44) authorises an applicant to remove the child to accommodation provided by the applicant or keep him or her there, or prevent

Previous legislation

Boarding-out

Boarding-out meant the placement of children by a local authority with foster carers, and was governed by Regulations, the most recent being the Boarding-out of Children (Foster Placement) Regulations 1988.

Access

Decisions about a parent's access to his or her child were governed by the local authority's duty to promote the long-term welfare of the child, and were subject to the Code of Practice on Access issued by the Secretary of State.

Application for a *Place of Safety Order* could be made to a single magistrate. The magistrate could authorise removal of the child to a place of safety for a maximum of 28 days.

removal from a hospital or other place. It can be made for a maximum of 8 days and can be extended once for a period of up to 7 days.

Police also have powers to protect children in emergencies.

Parental responsibility

Parental responsibility is defined under s.3(1) of the Act as "all the rights, duties, powers and responsibilities which by law a parent has in relation to a child and his property."

Parental responsibility can be shared, and is only extinguished by adoption.

Preventive duty

Local authorities are under a statutory duty under s.17 of the Act to safeguard and promote the welfare of children in their area who are in need and, so far as is consistent with their welfare, to promote their upbringing by their families.

Under the Child Care Act 1980, s.1, local authorities were under a statutory duty to diminish the need to receive children into their care or keep them in care by giving advice, guidance and assistance.

Wardship

The Children Act 1989 places limits on the way in which wardship may be used. A child who is subject to a care order may not be made a ward. A local authority may not use wardship and may only use the inherent jurisdiction of the High Court with the leave of the court in exceptional circumstances.

Application can be made under the Guardianship of Minors Act 1971 to ward any child under the age of 18. Once warded the child's custody vests in the court, which becomes in effect their legal parent.